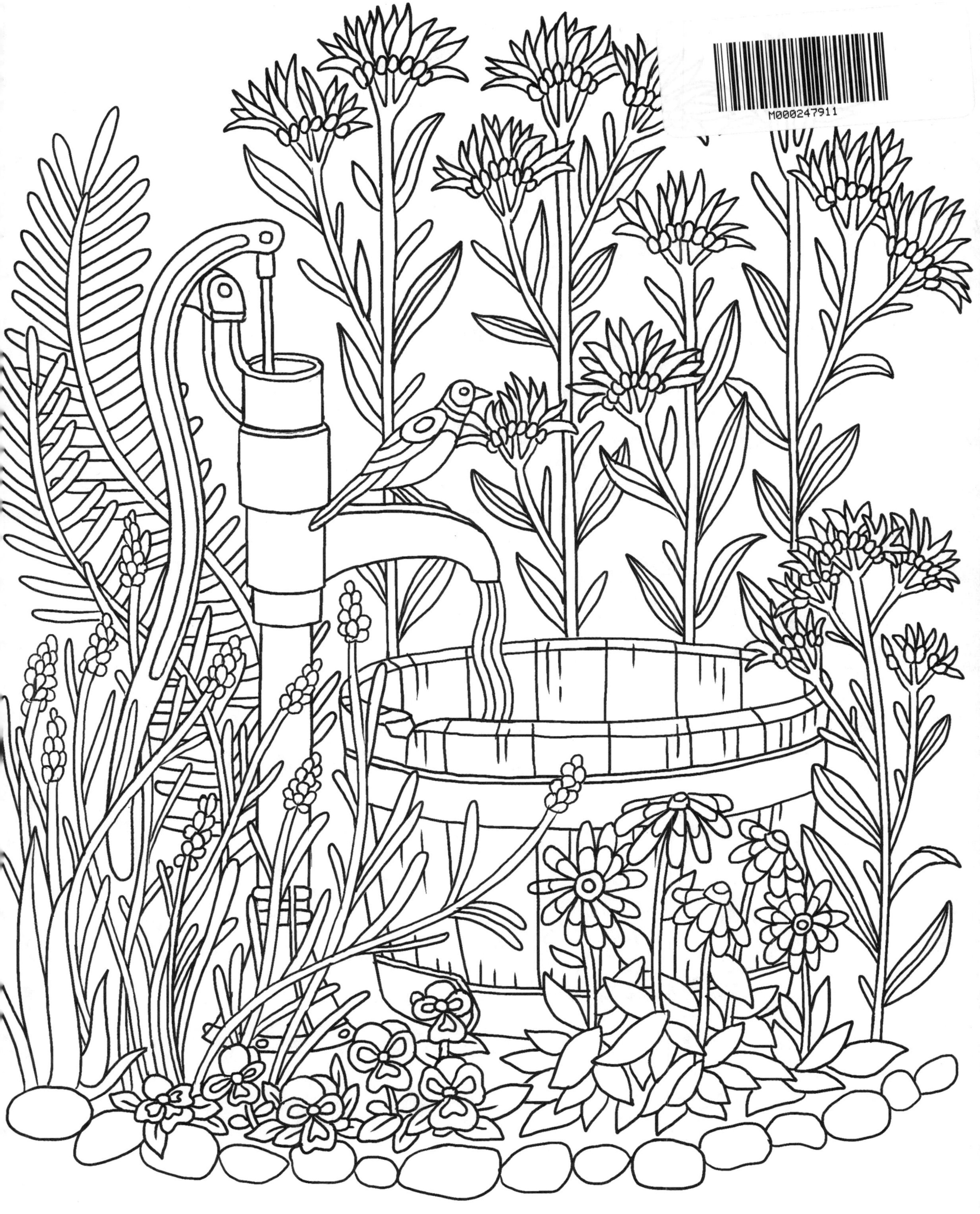

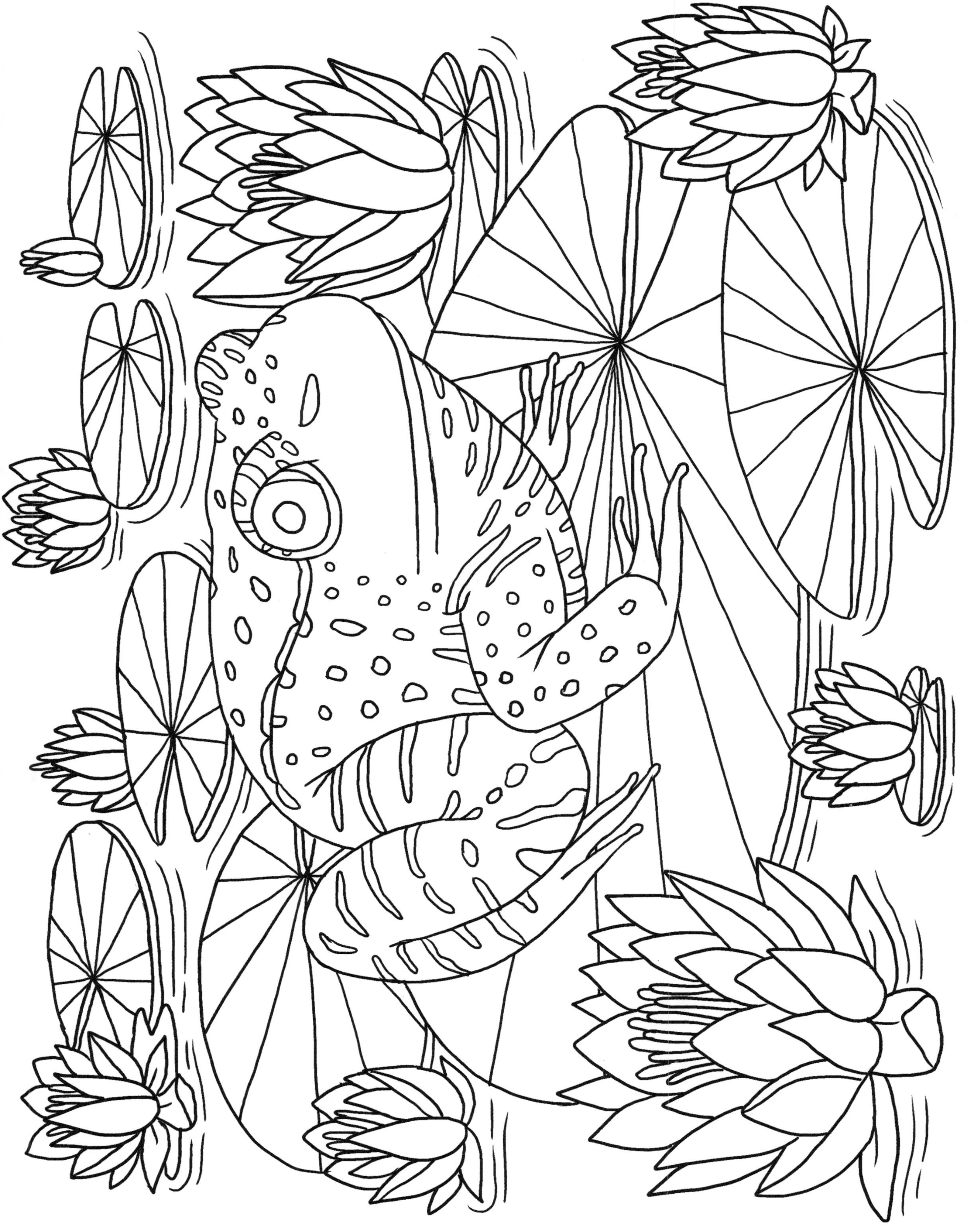

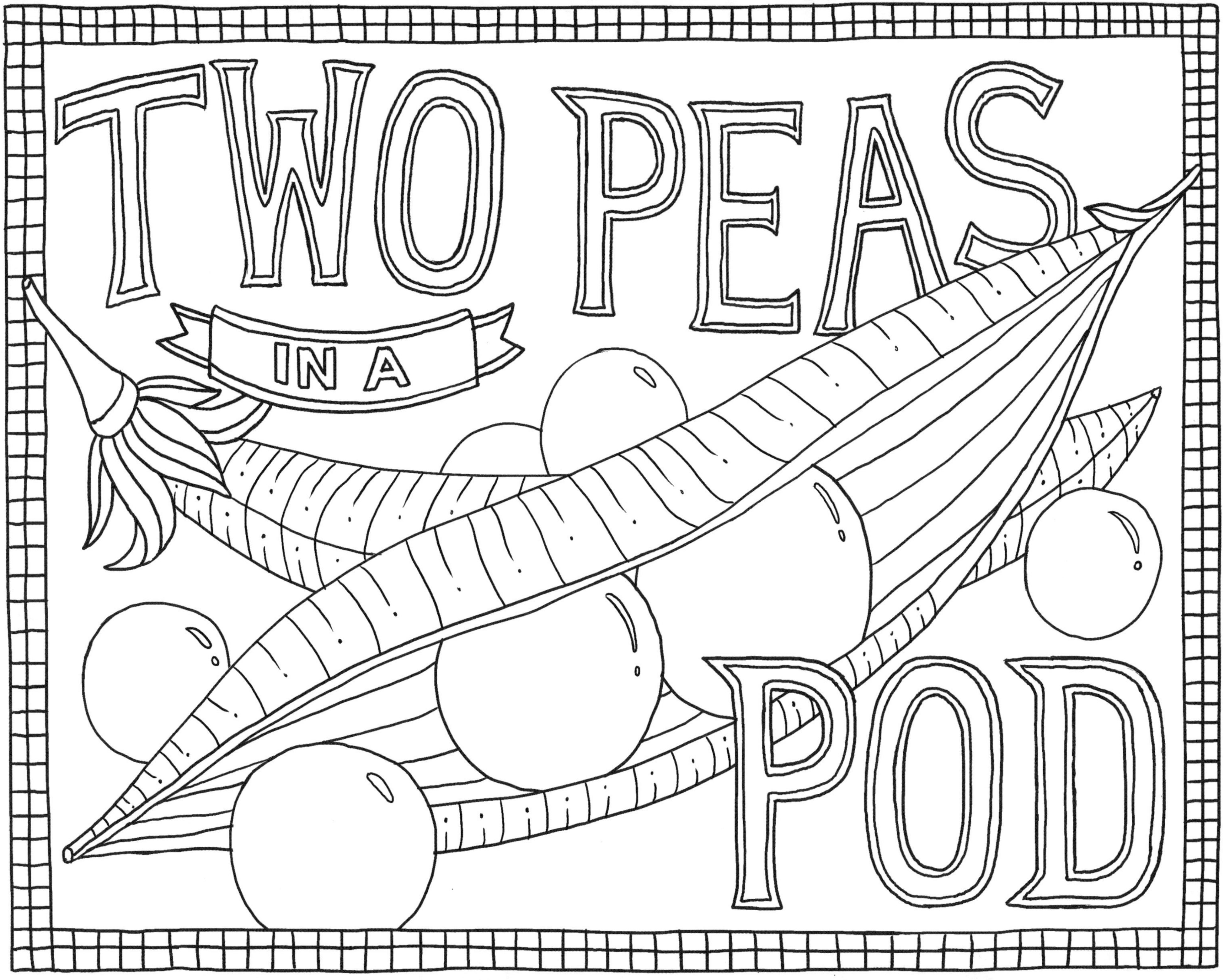
TWO PEAS
IN A
POD

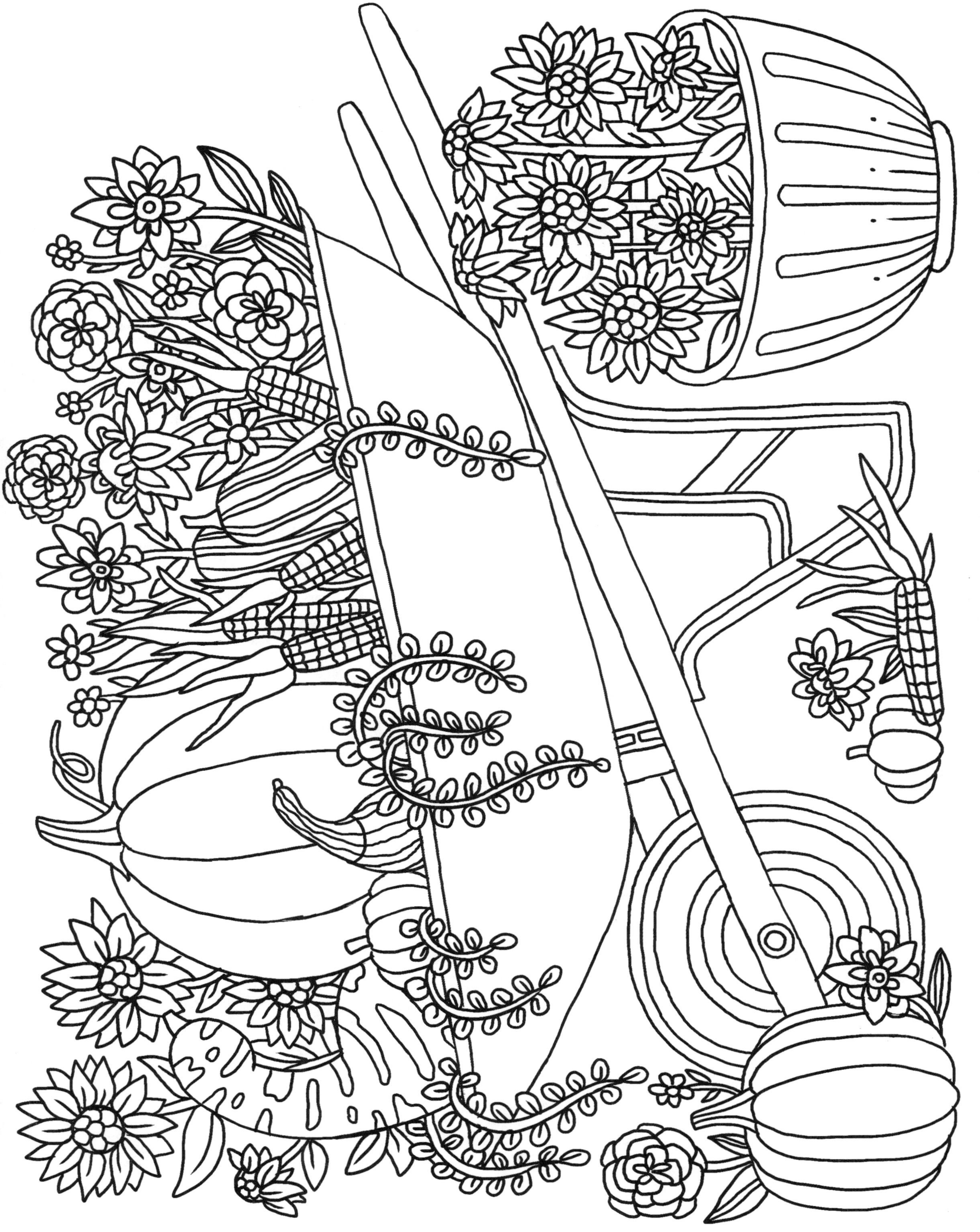

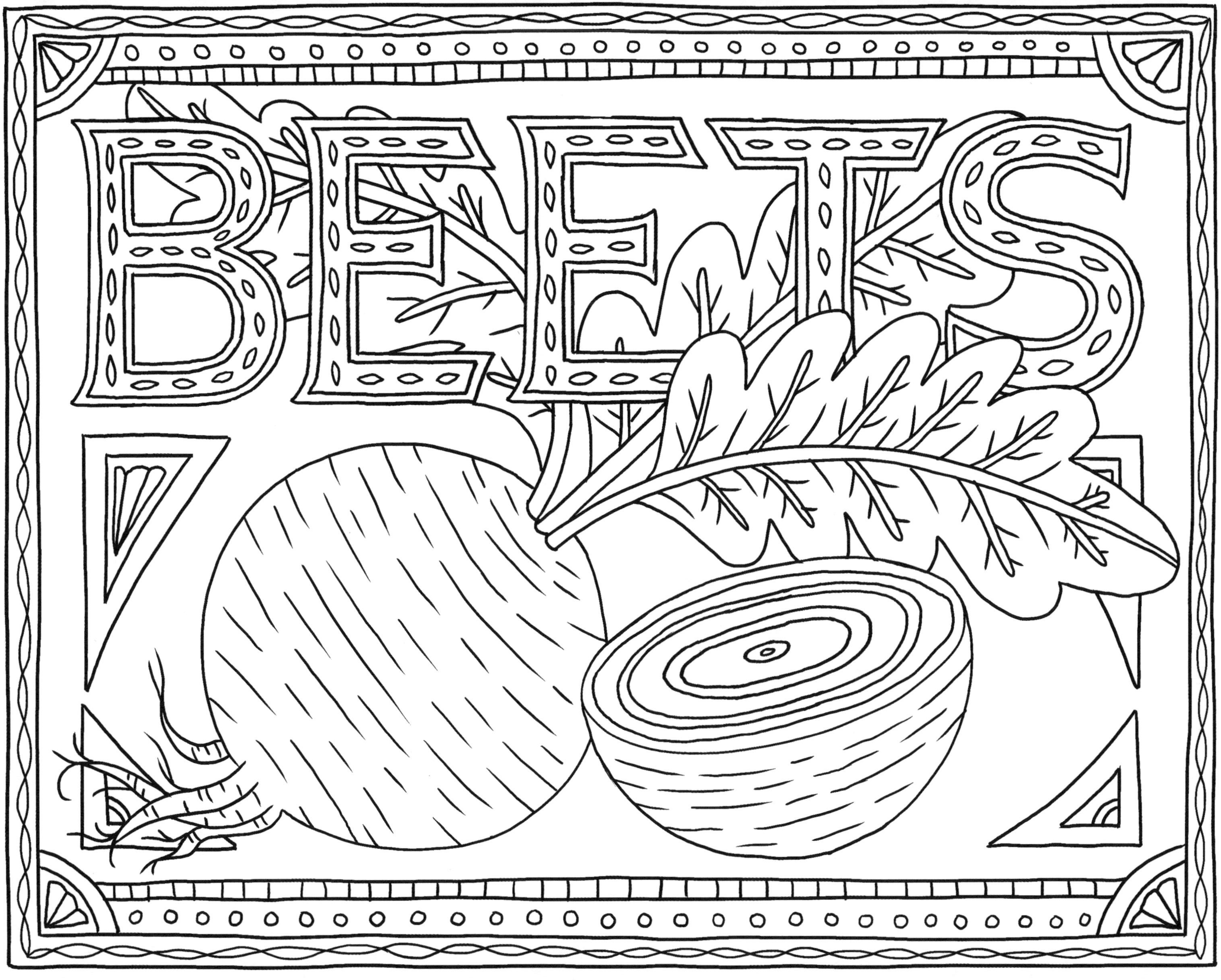
BEETS

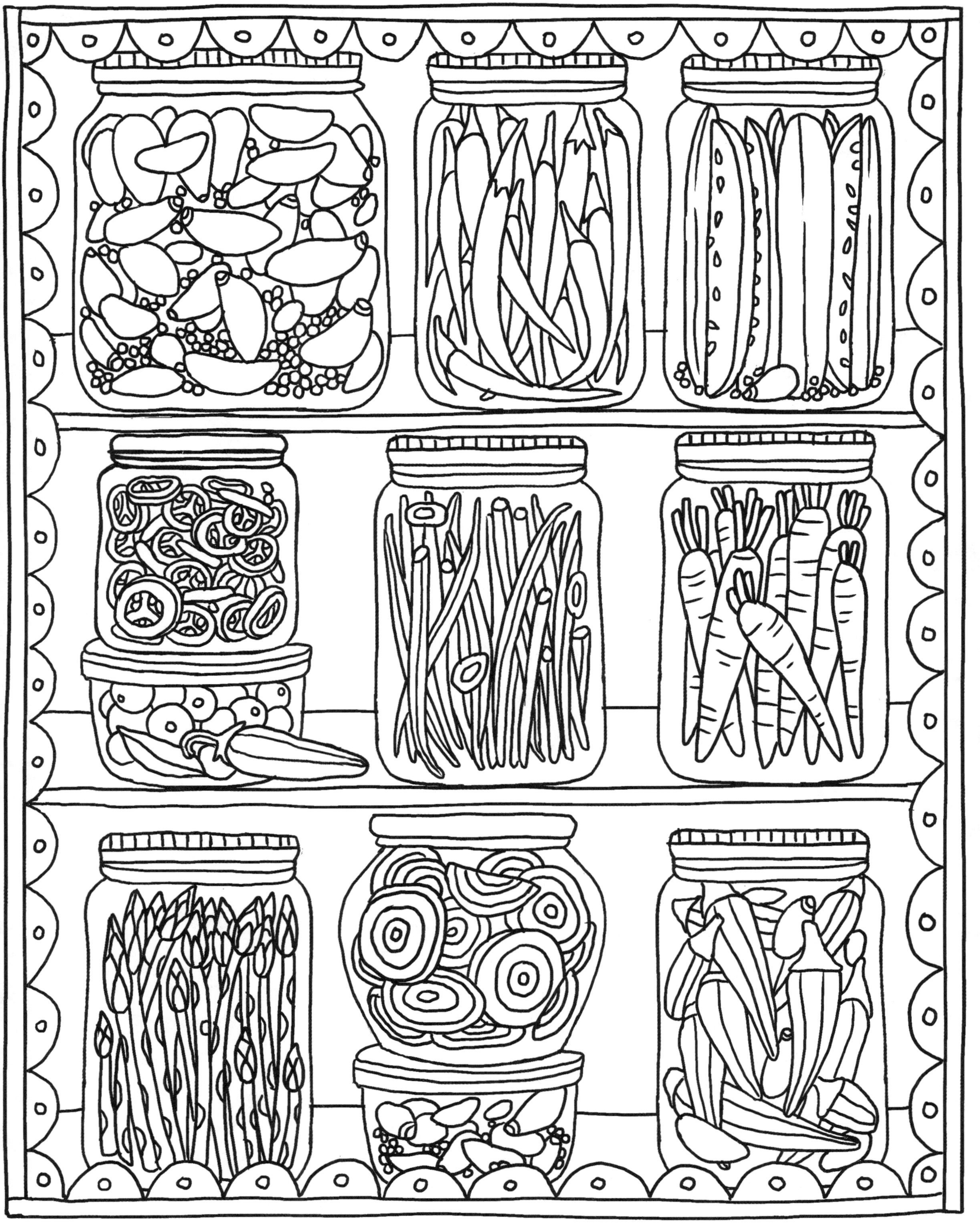

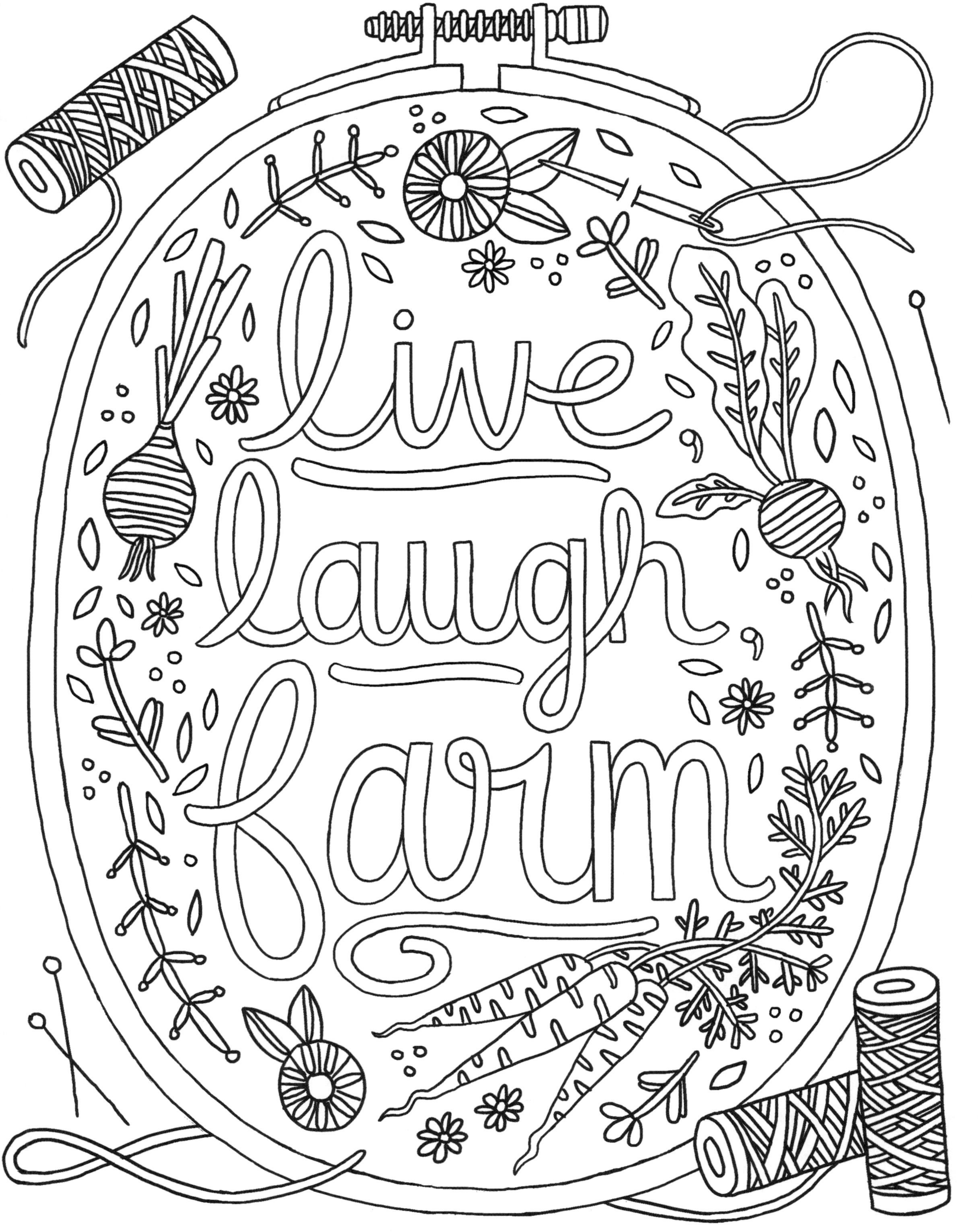
live, laugh, farm

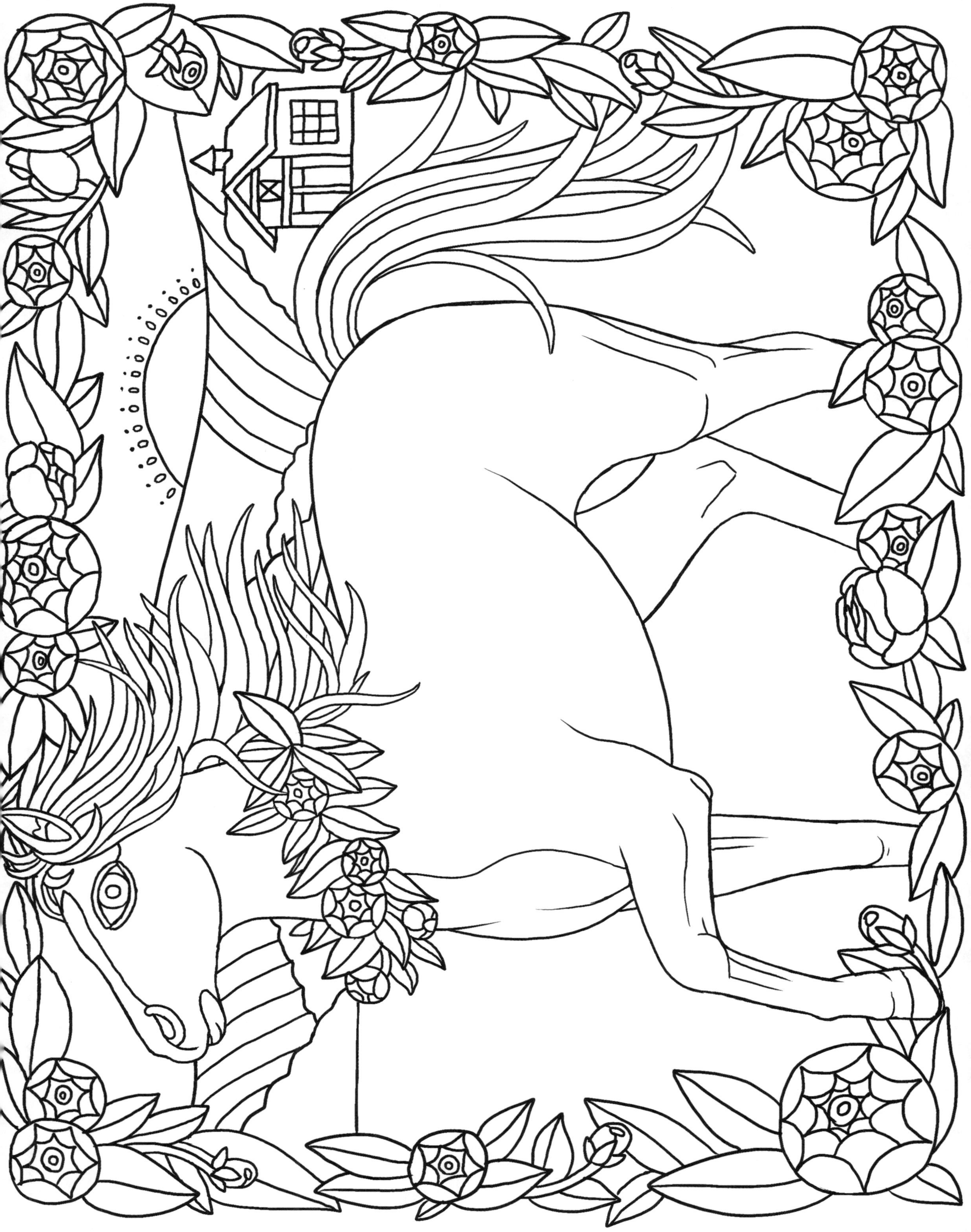

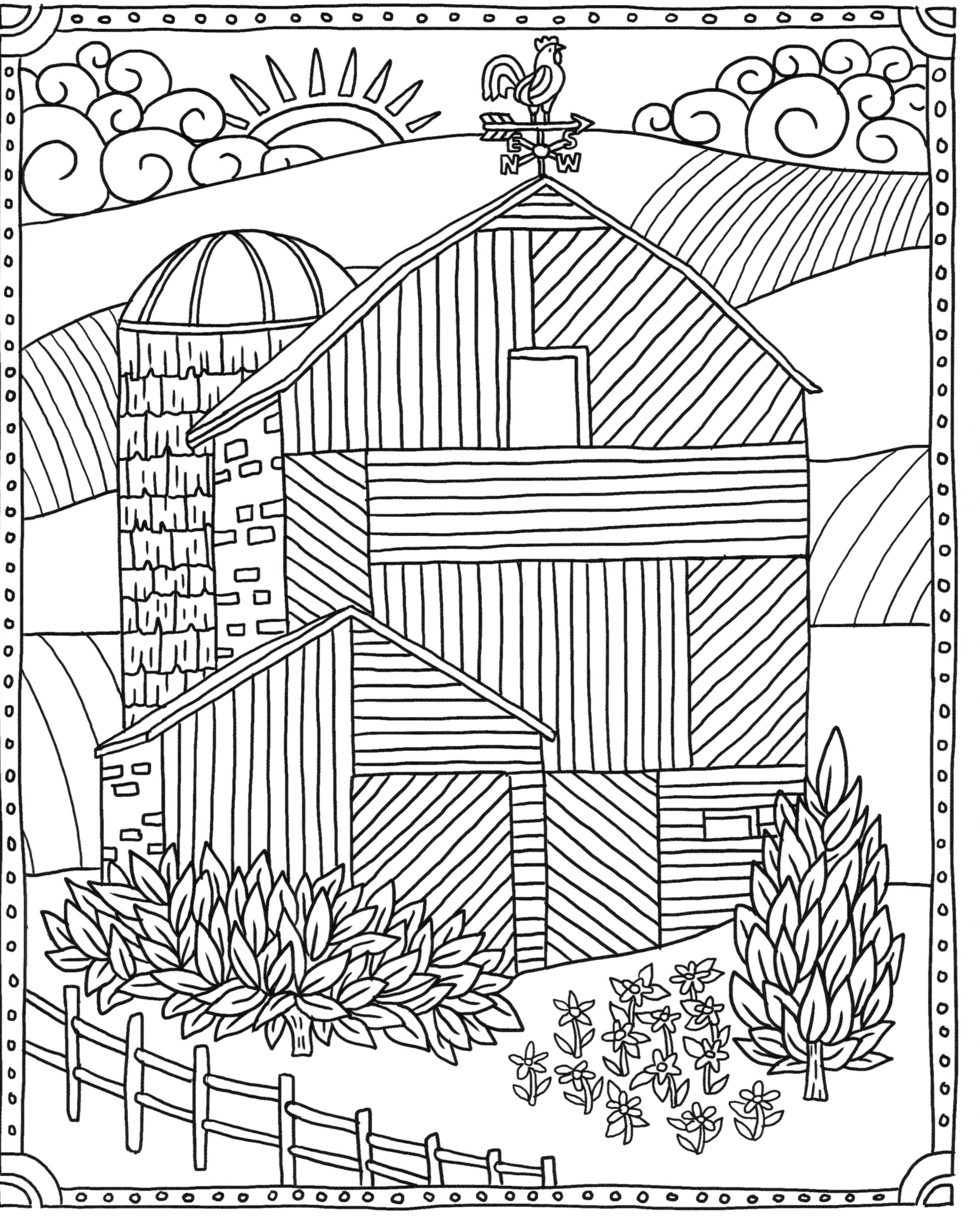
E S
N W

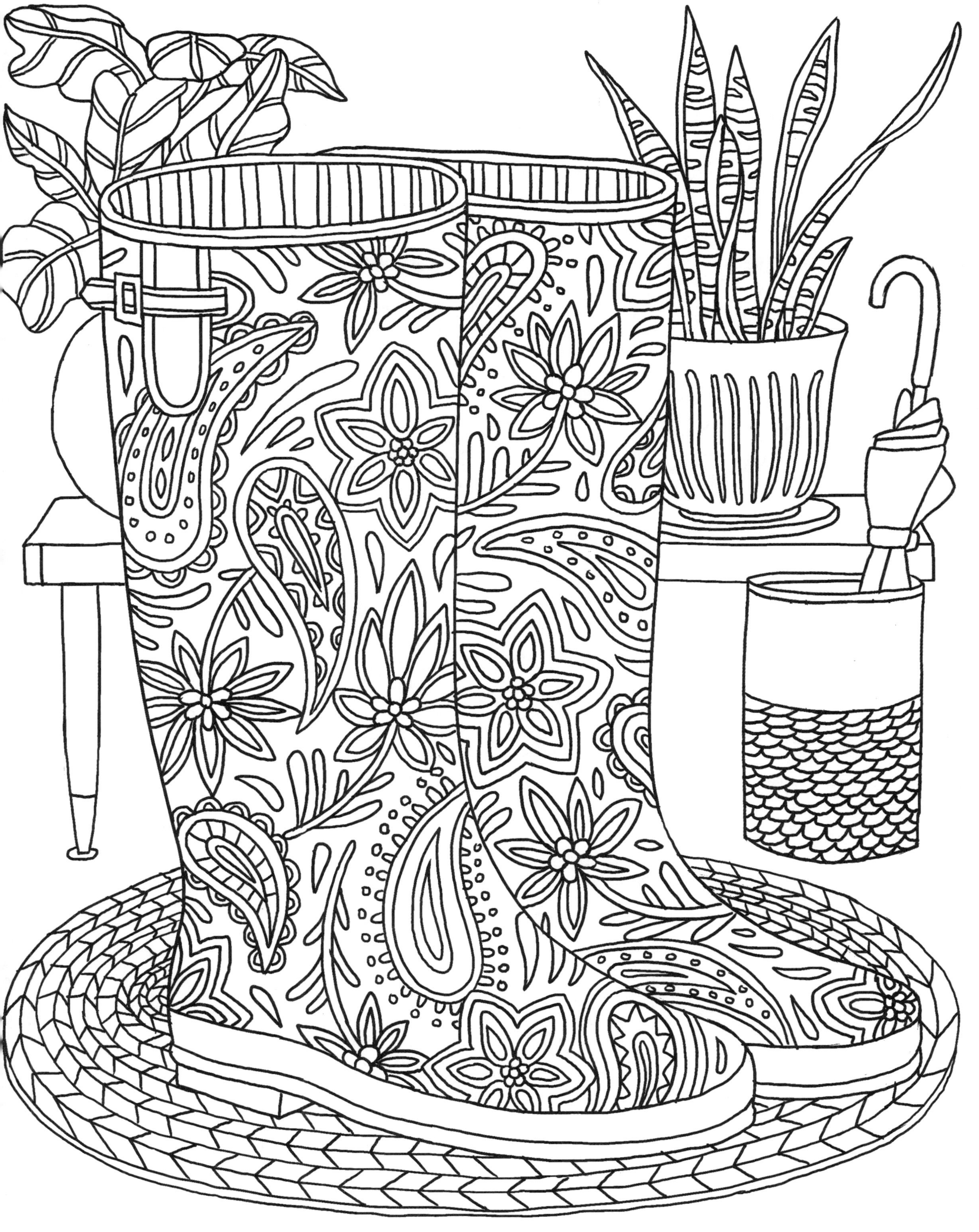

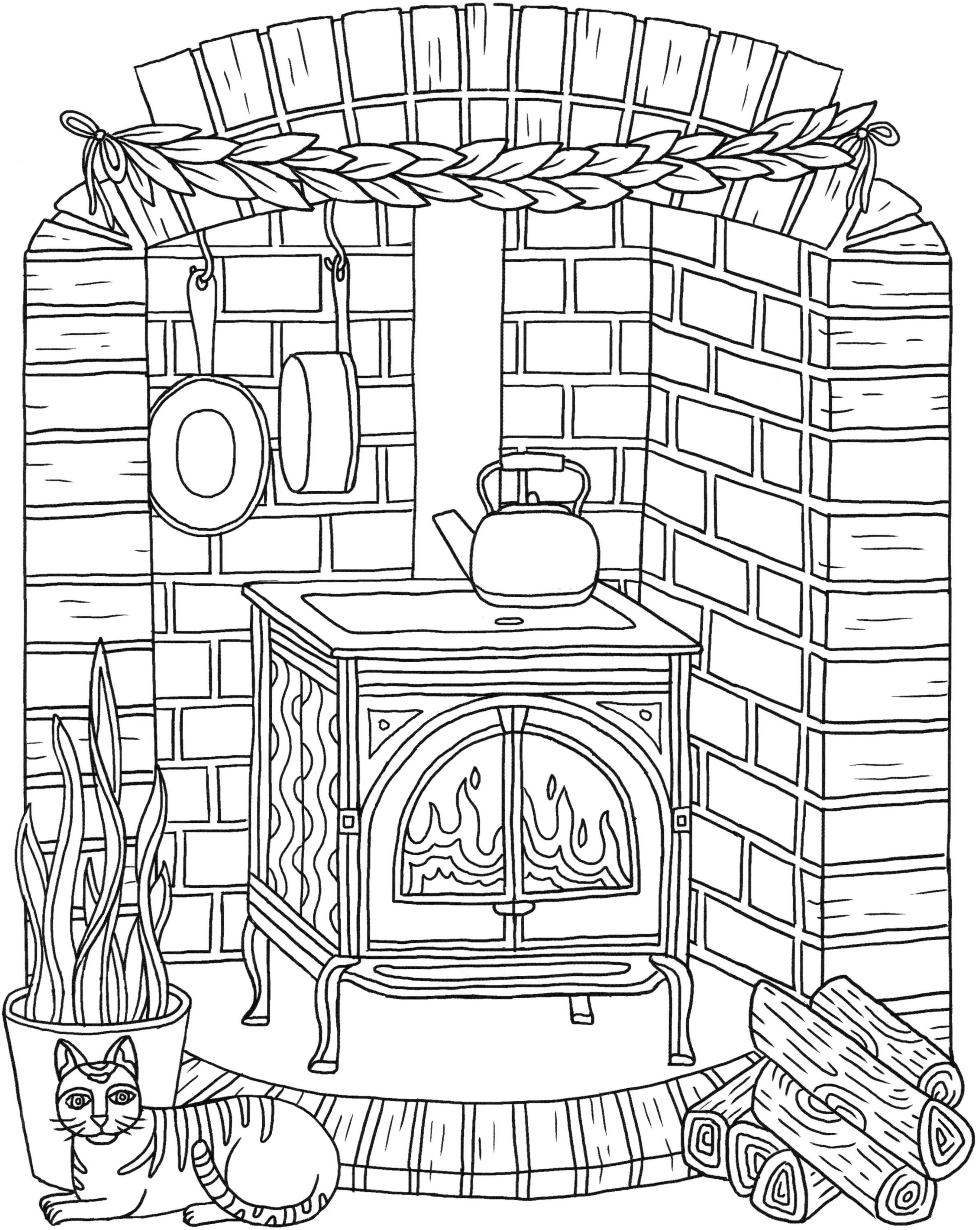

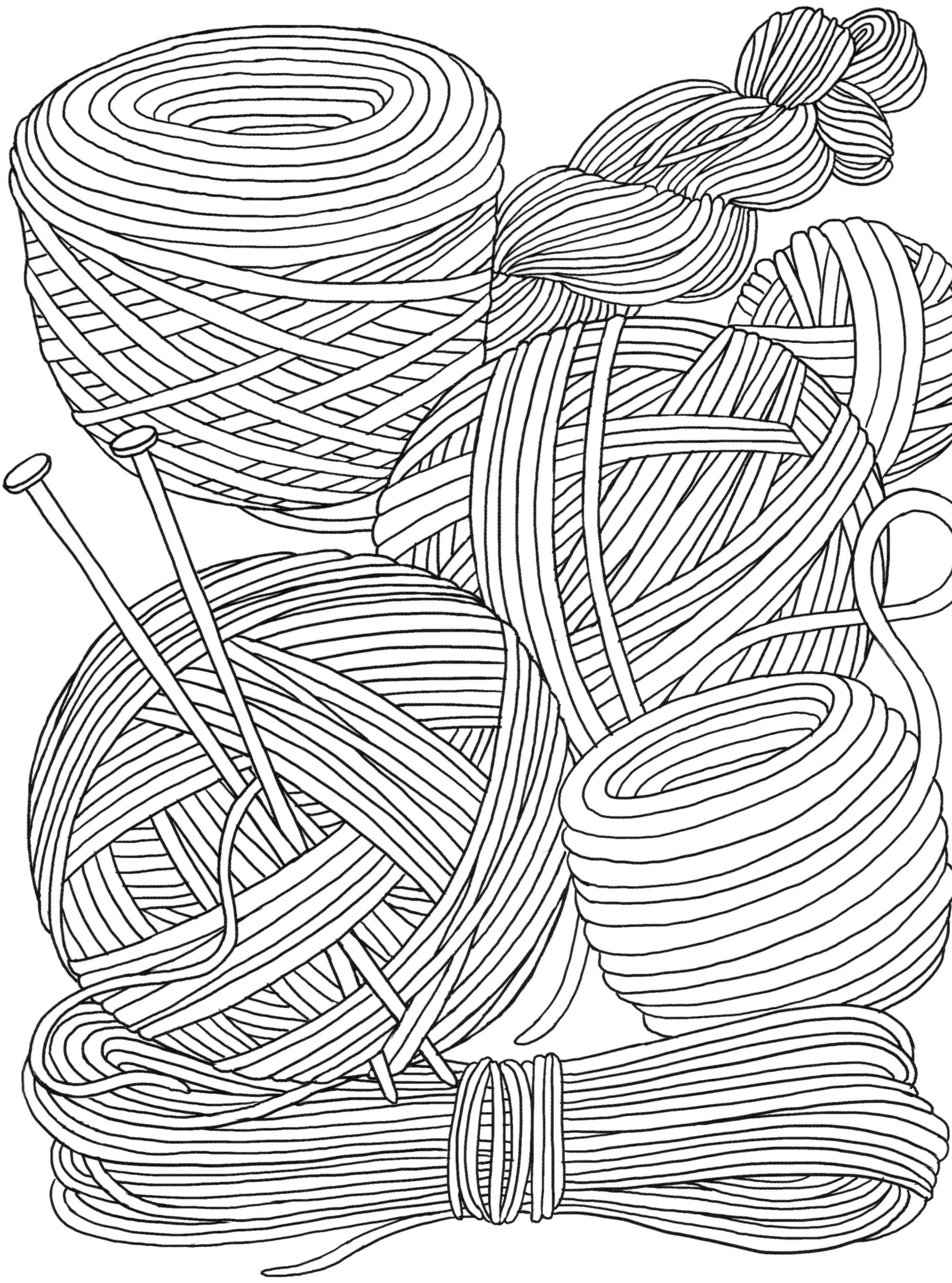

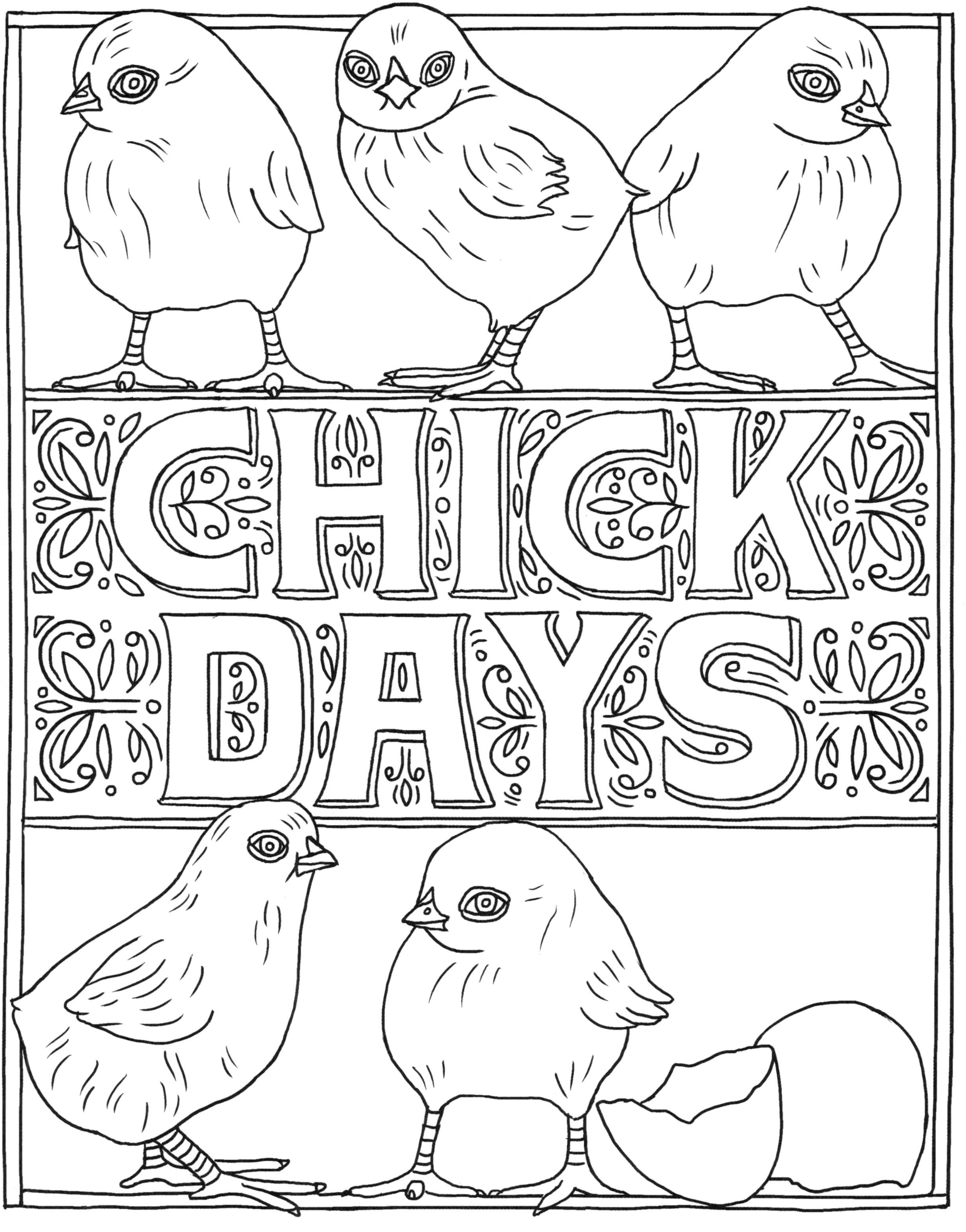
CHICK
DAYS

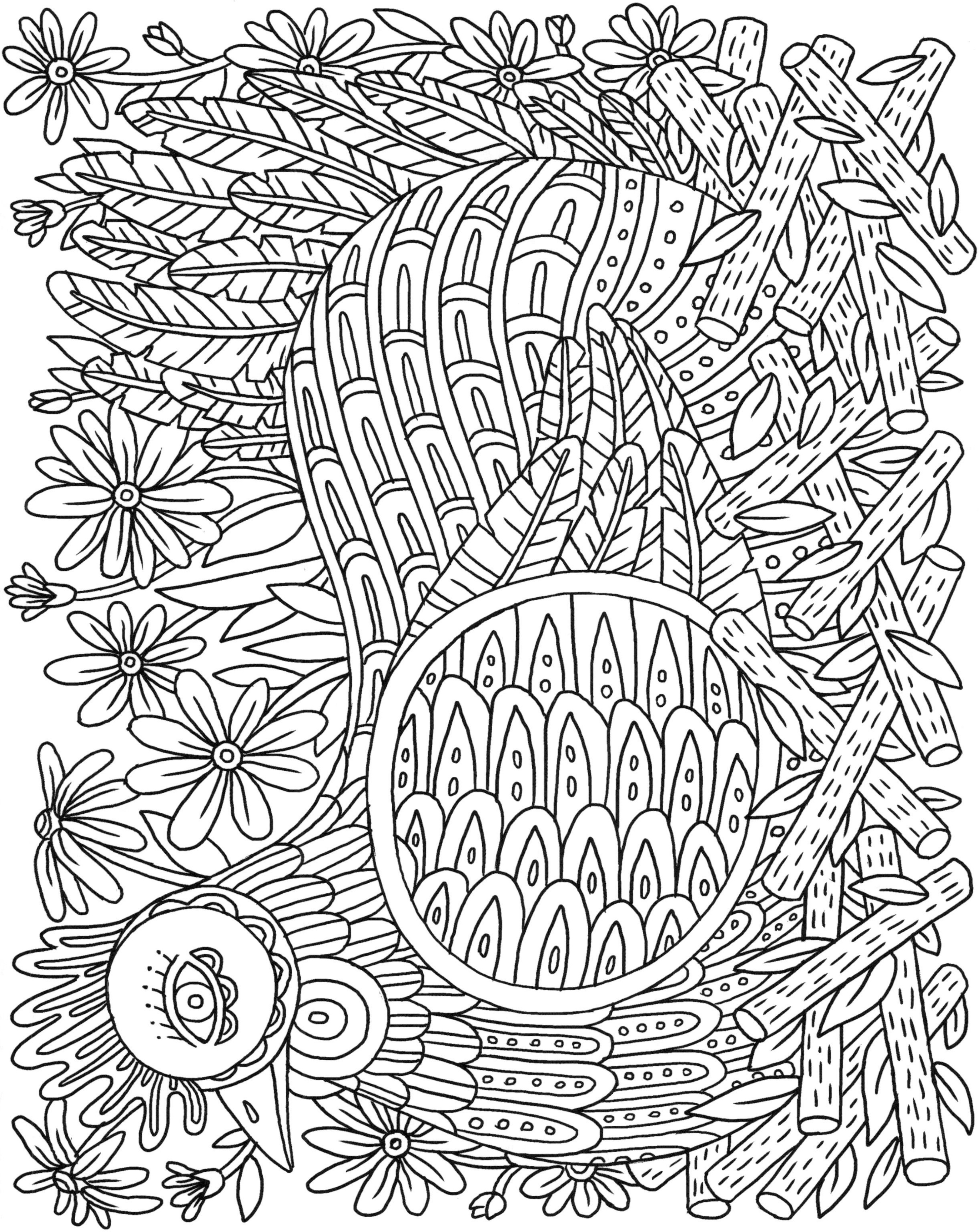

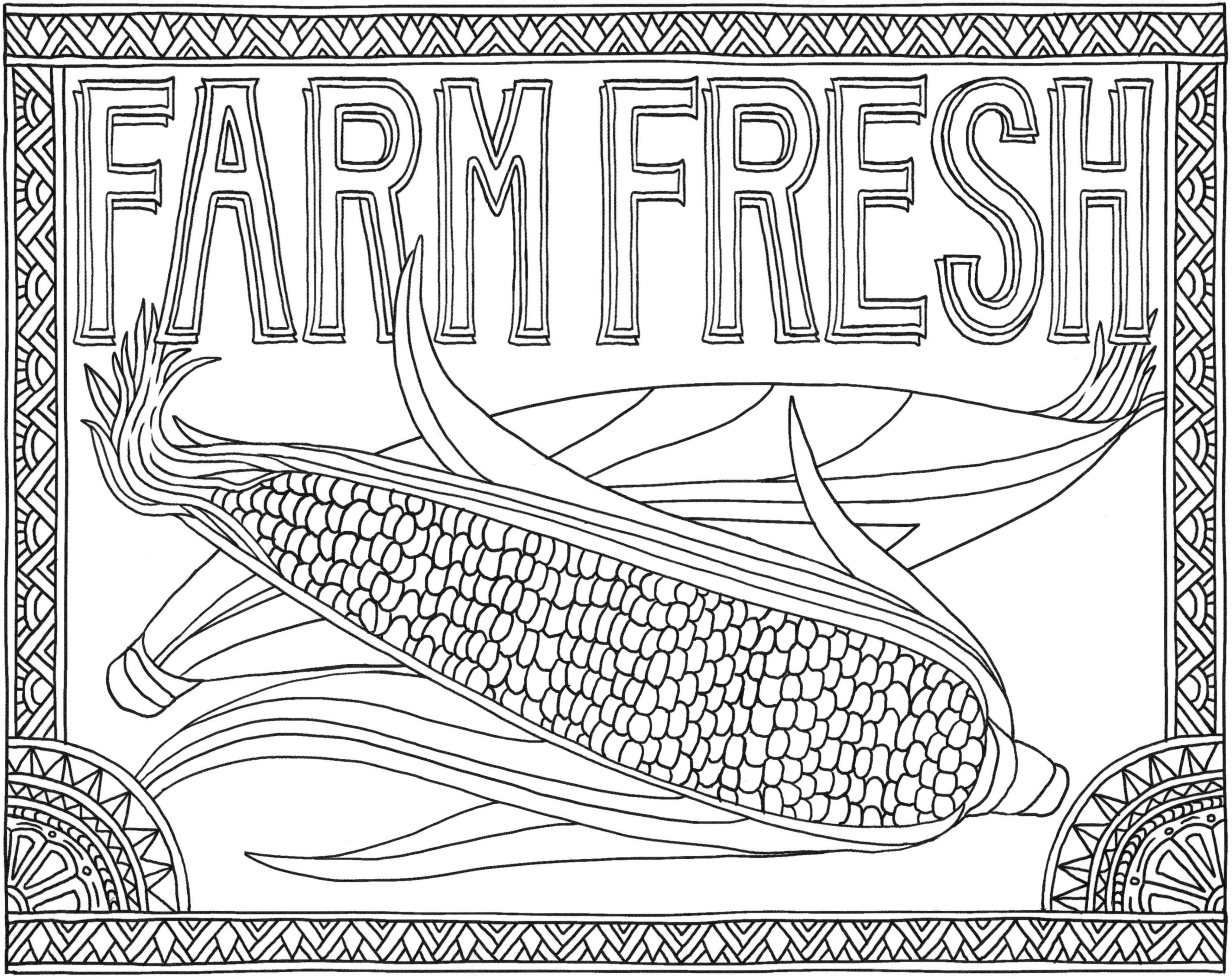
FARM FRESH

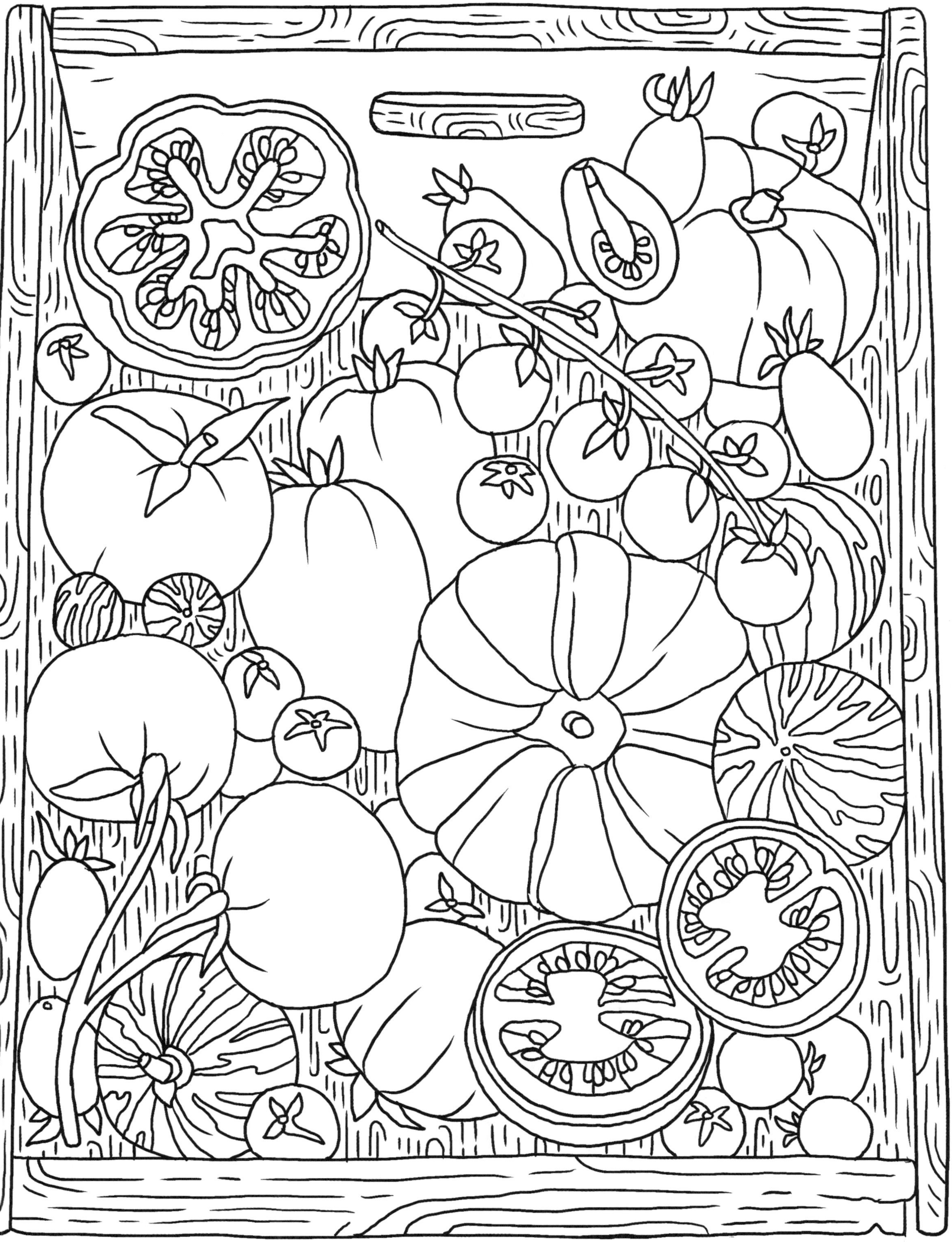

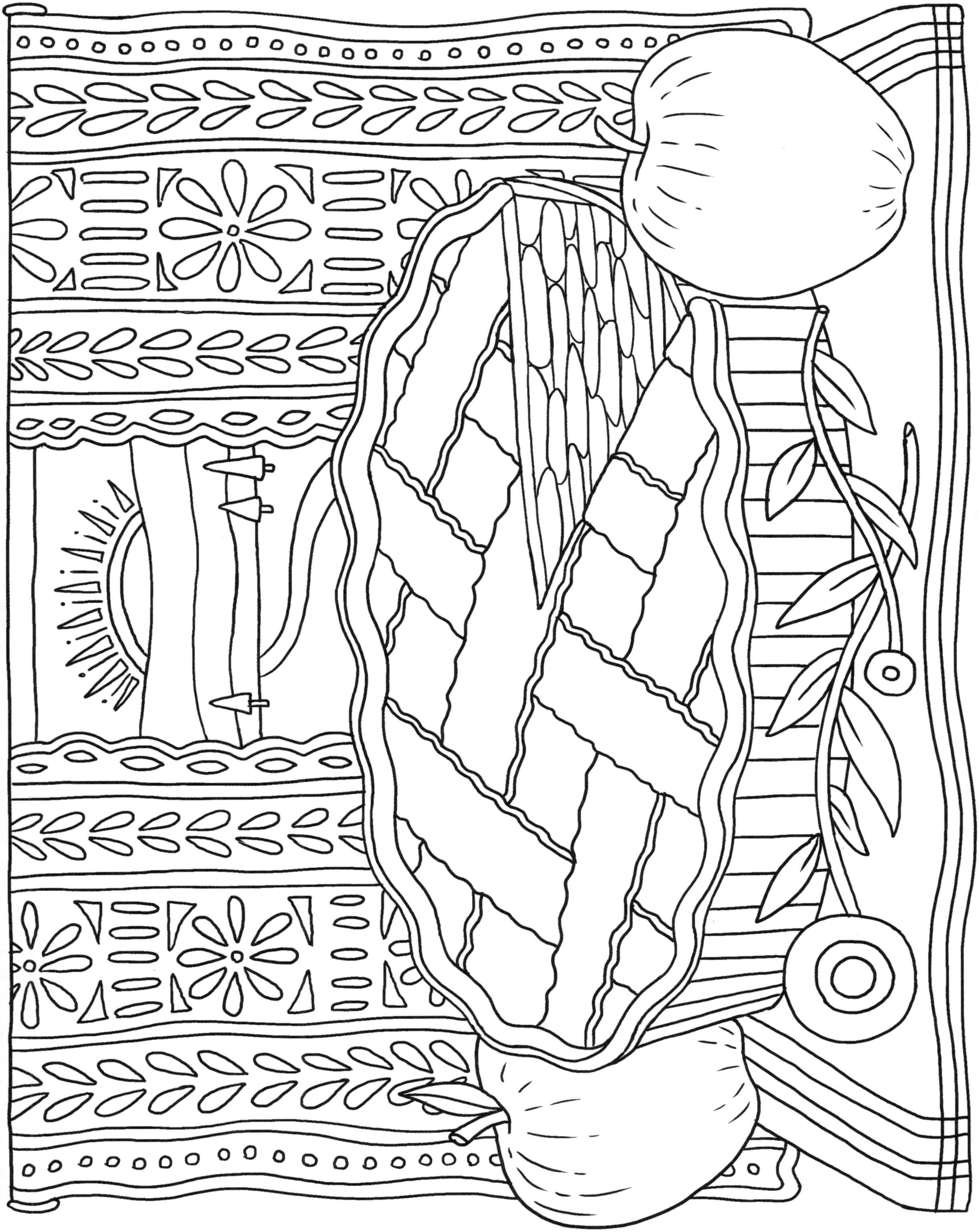

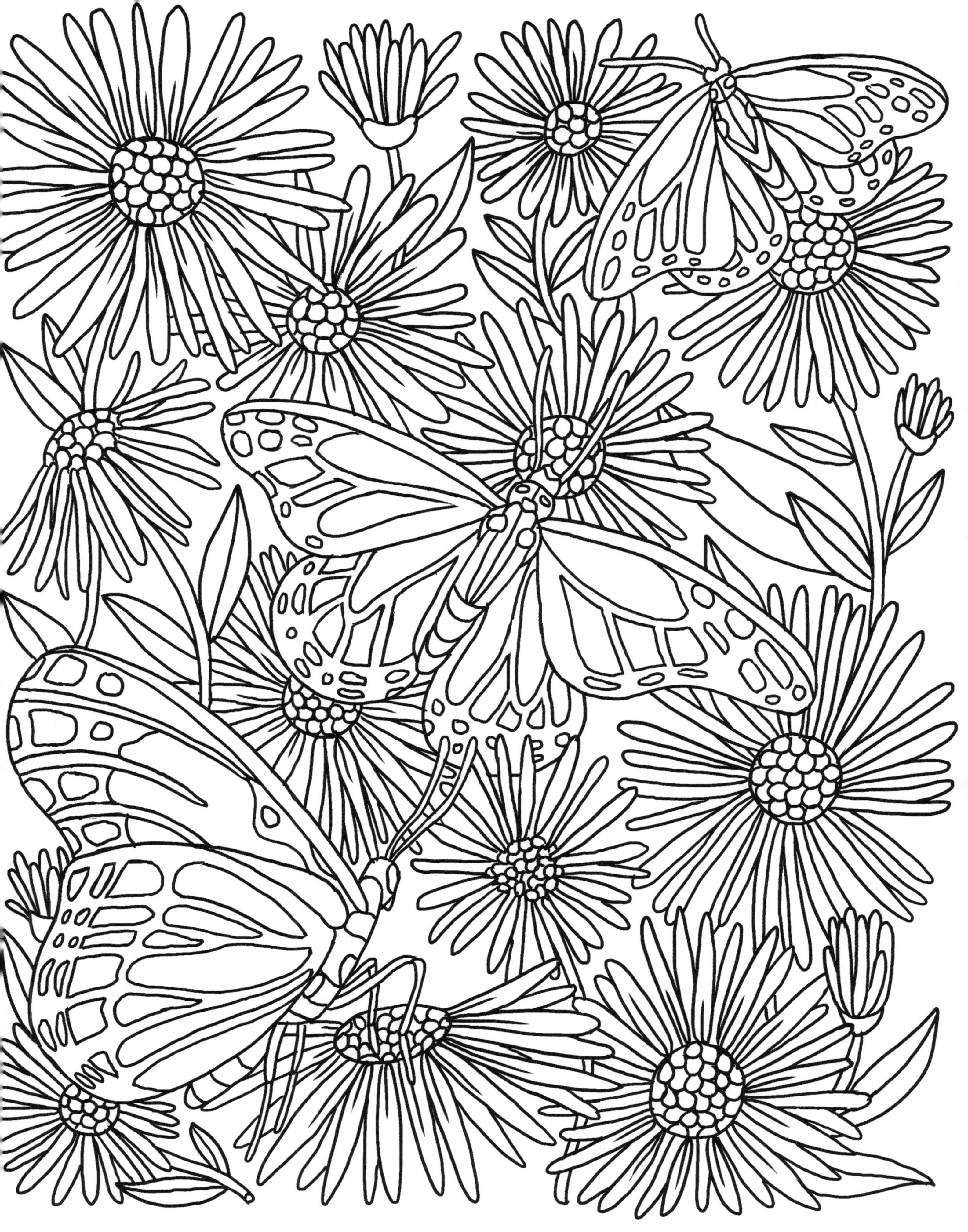

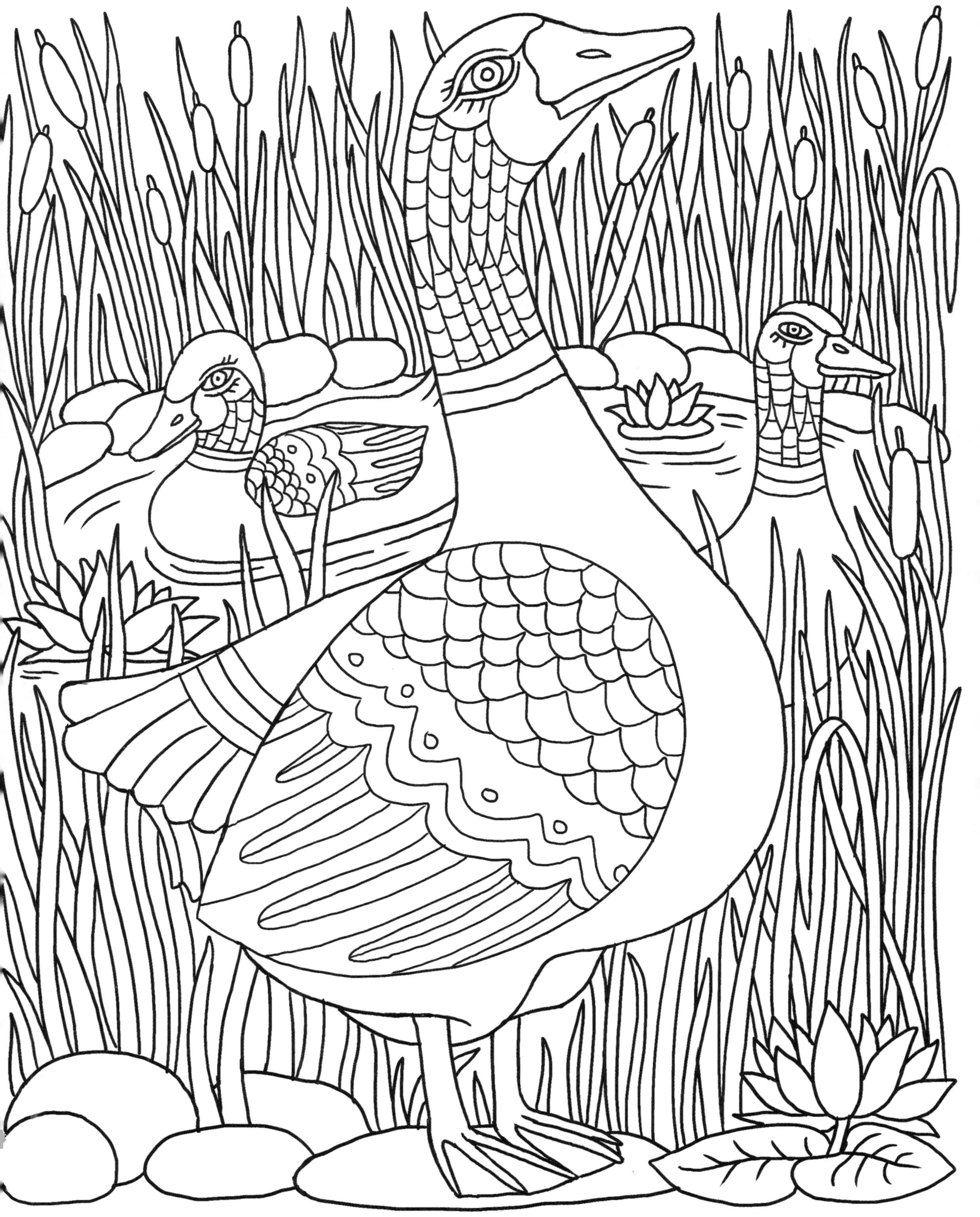

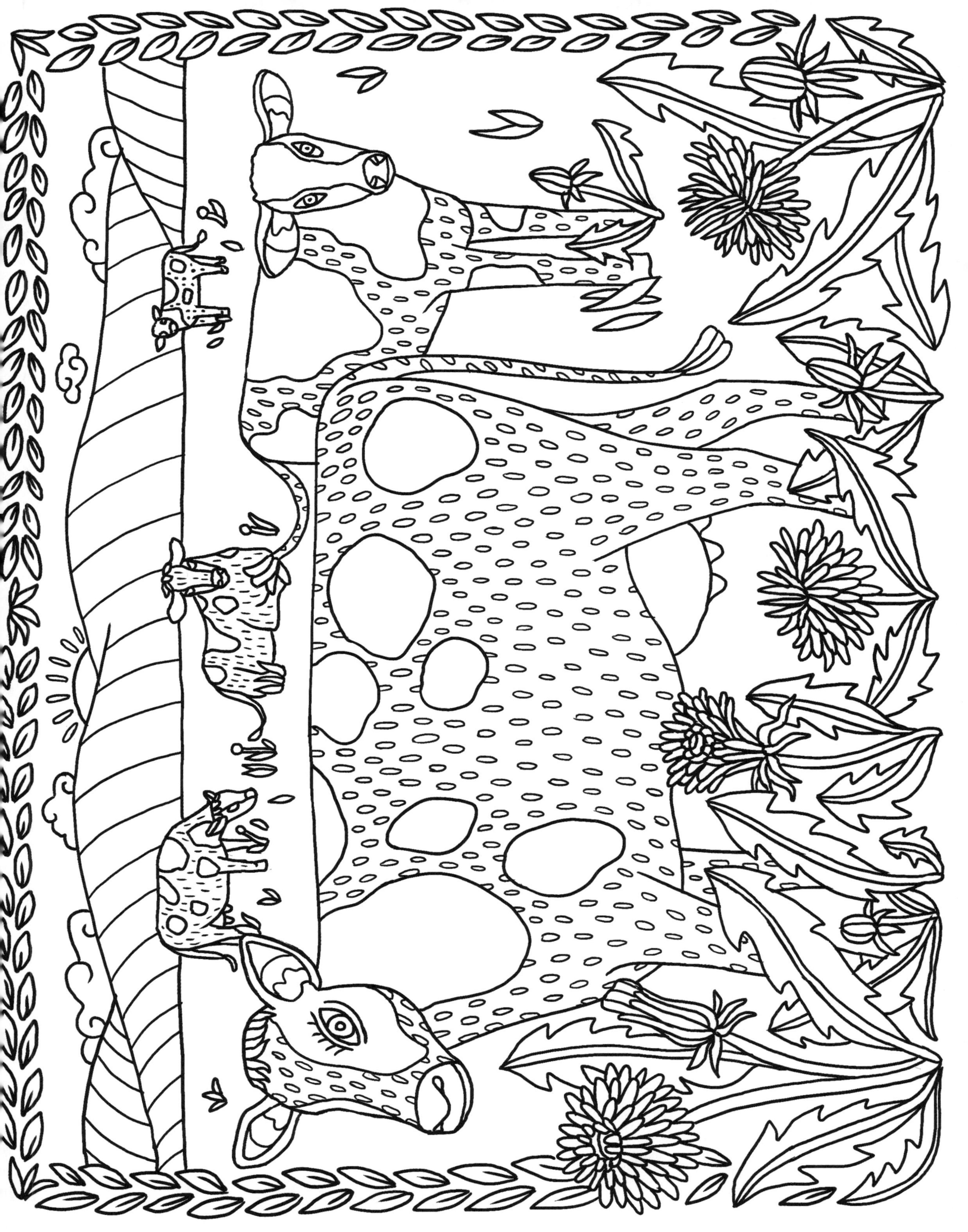

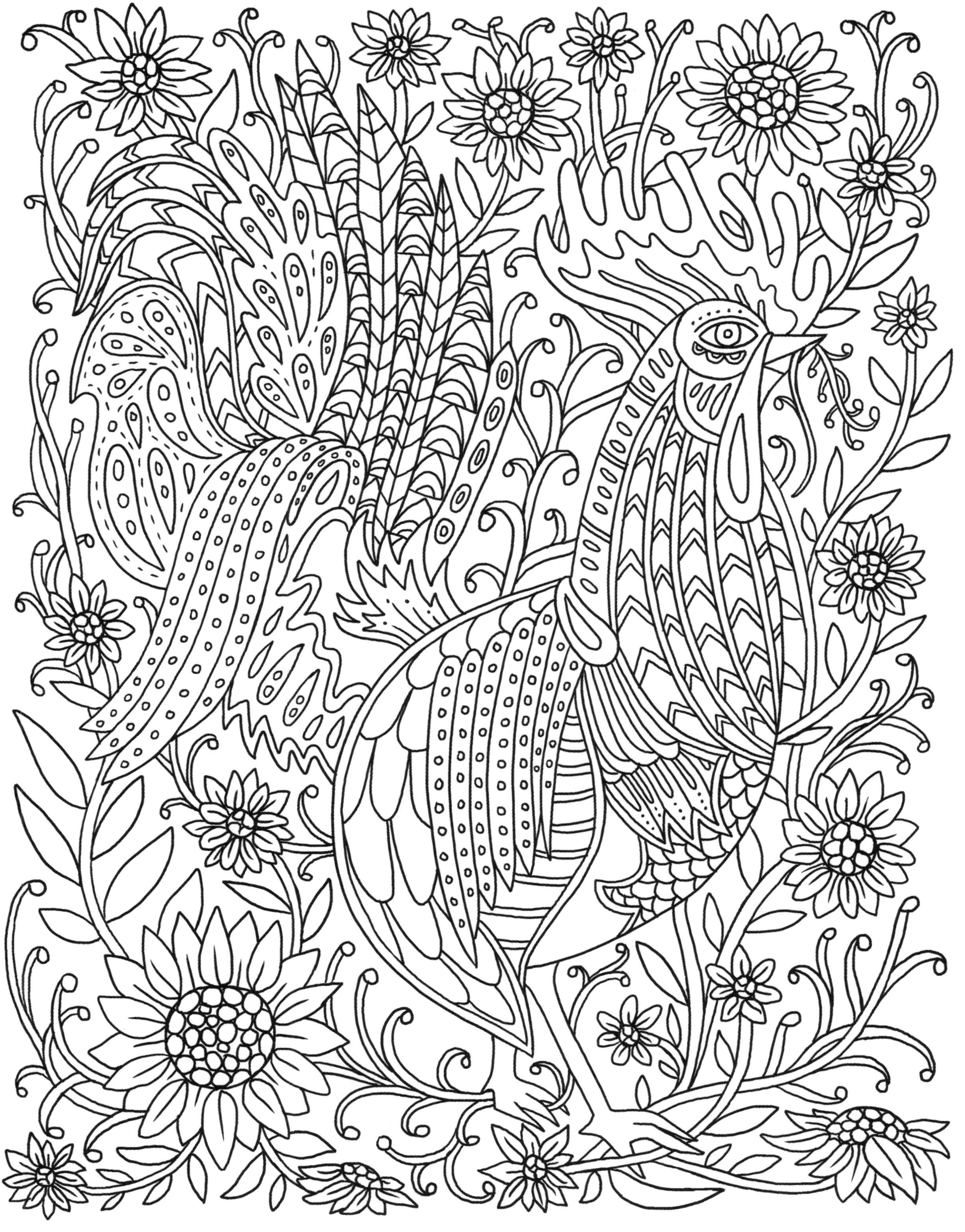

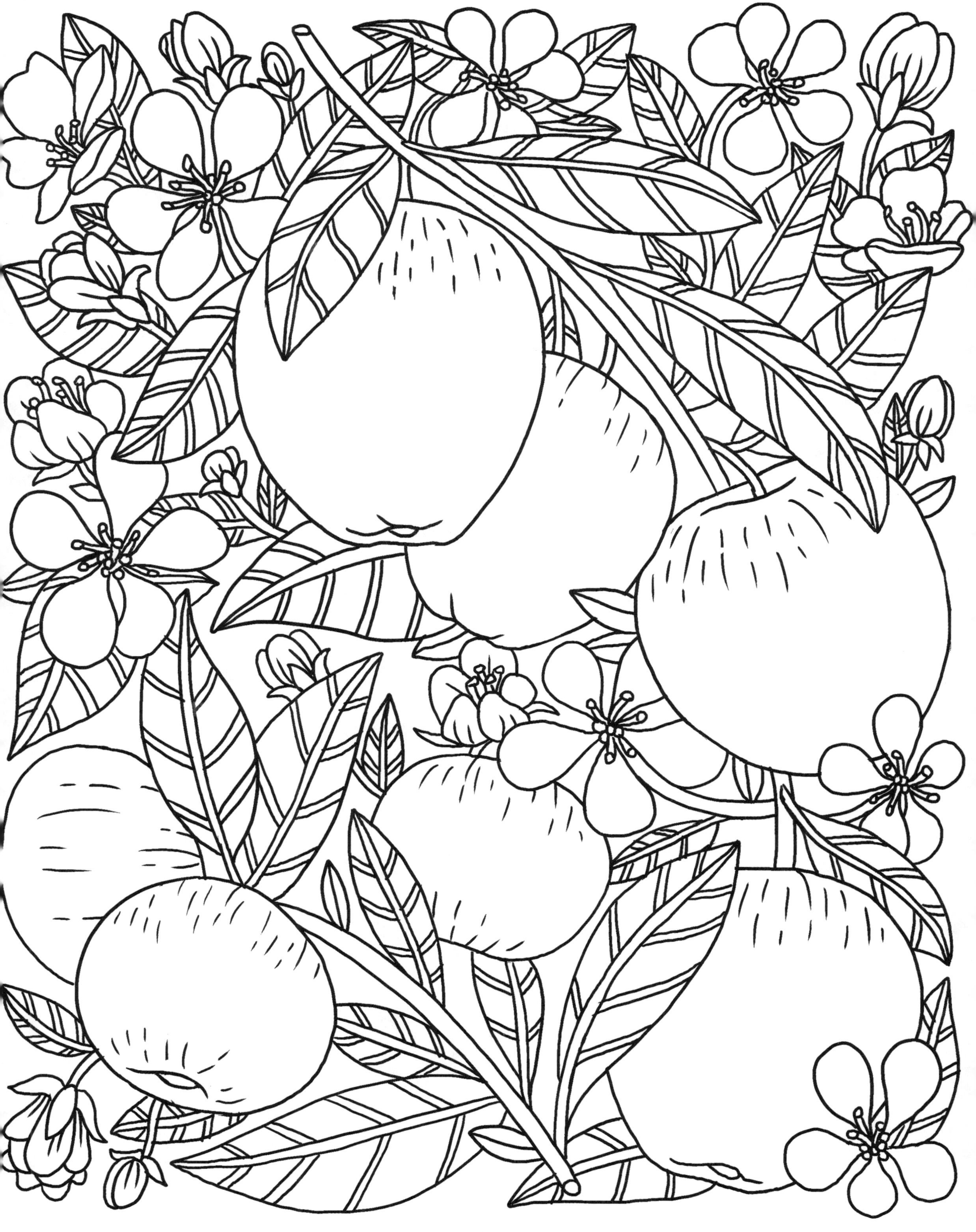

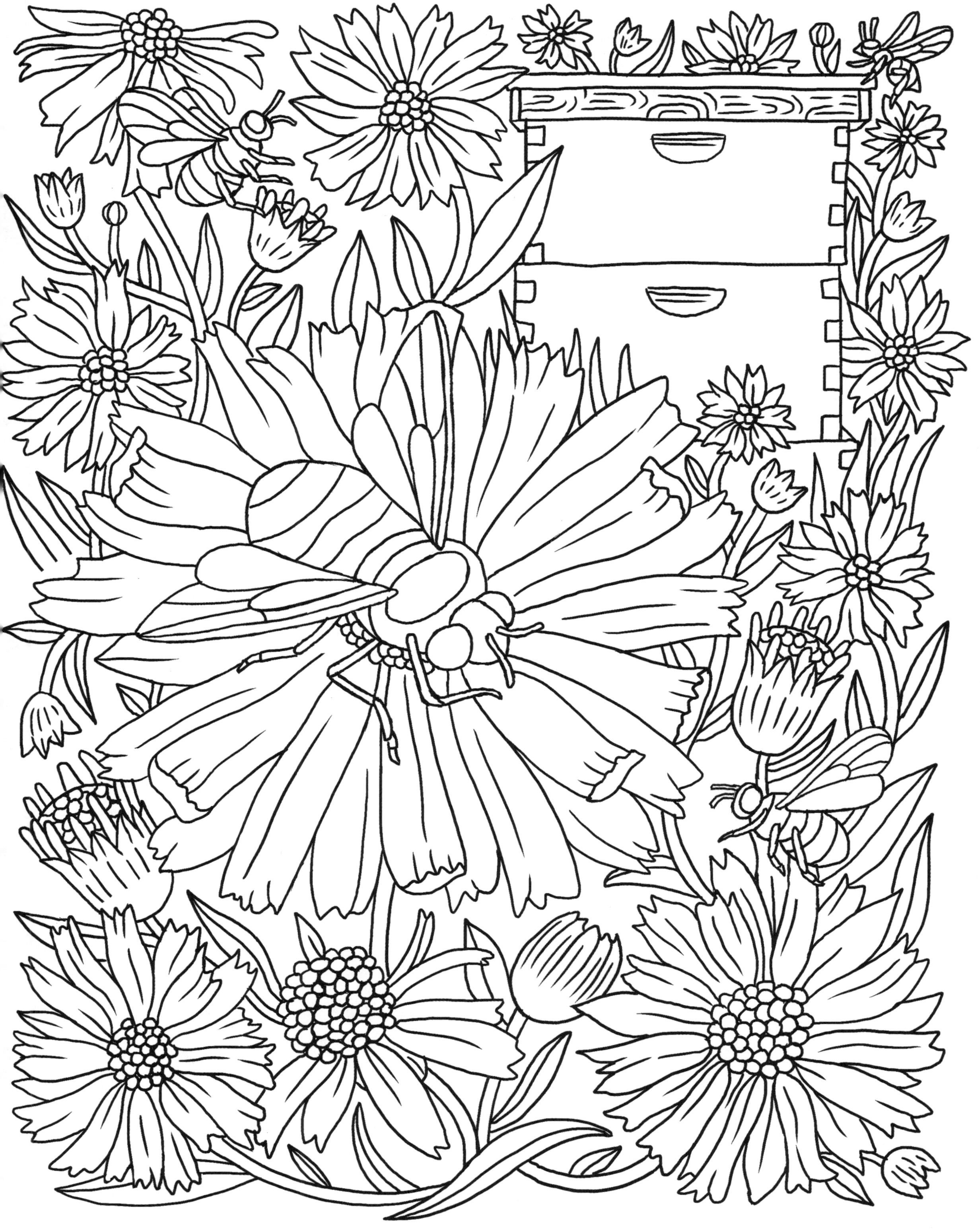

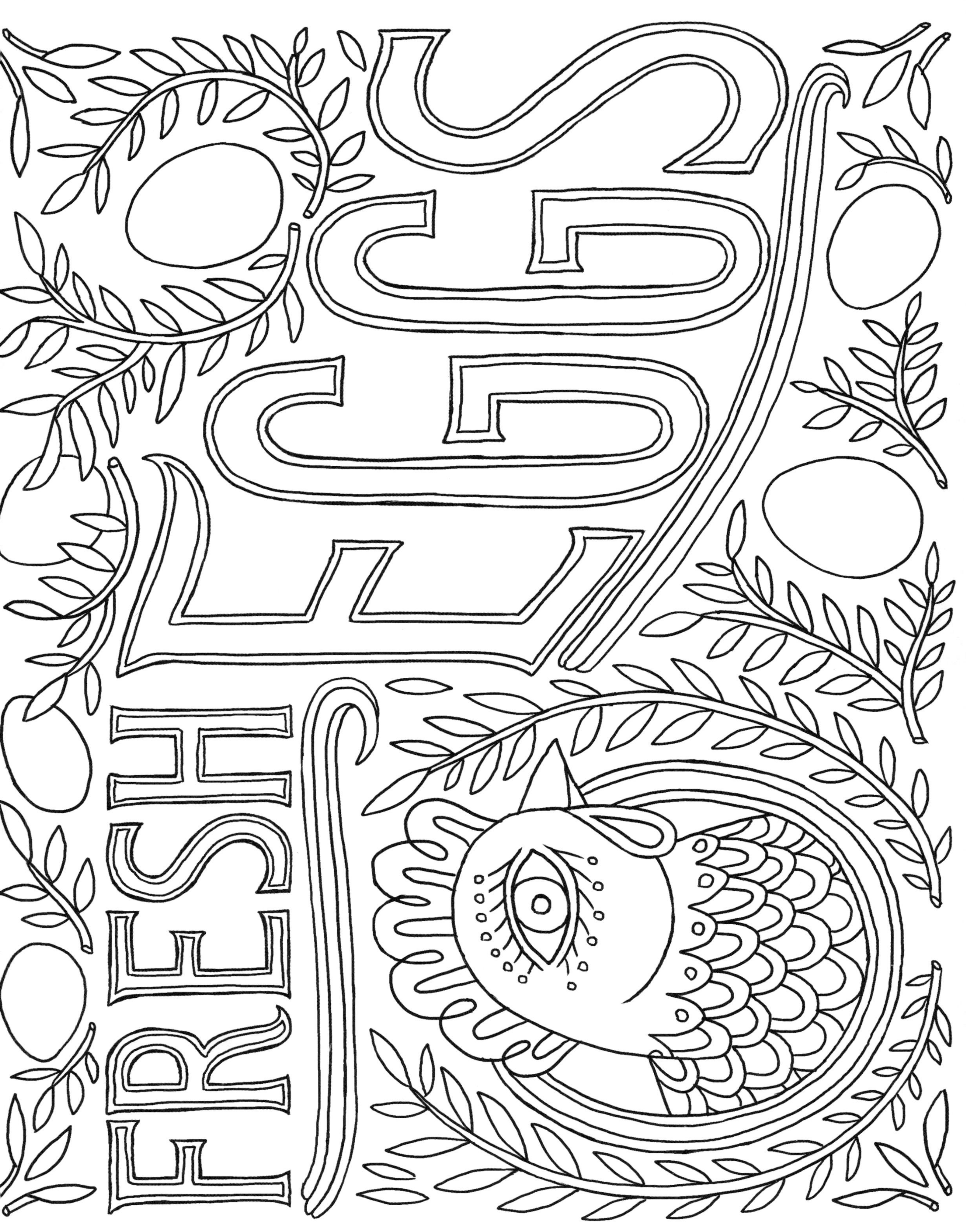
FRESH EGGS

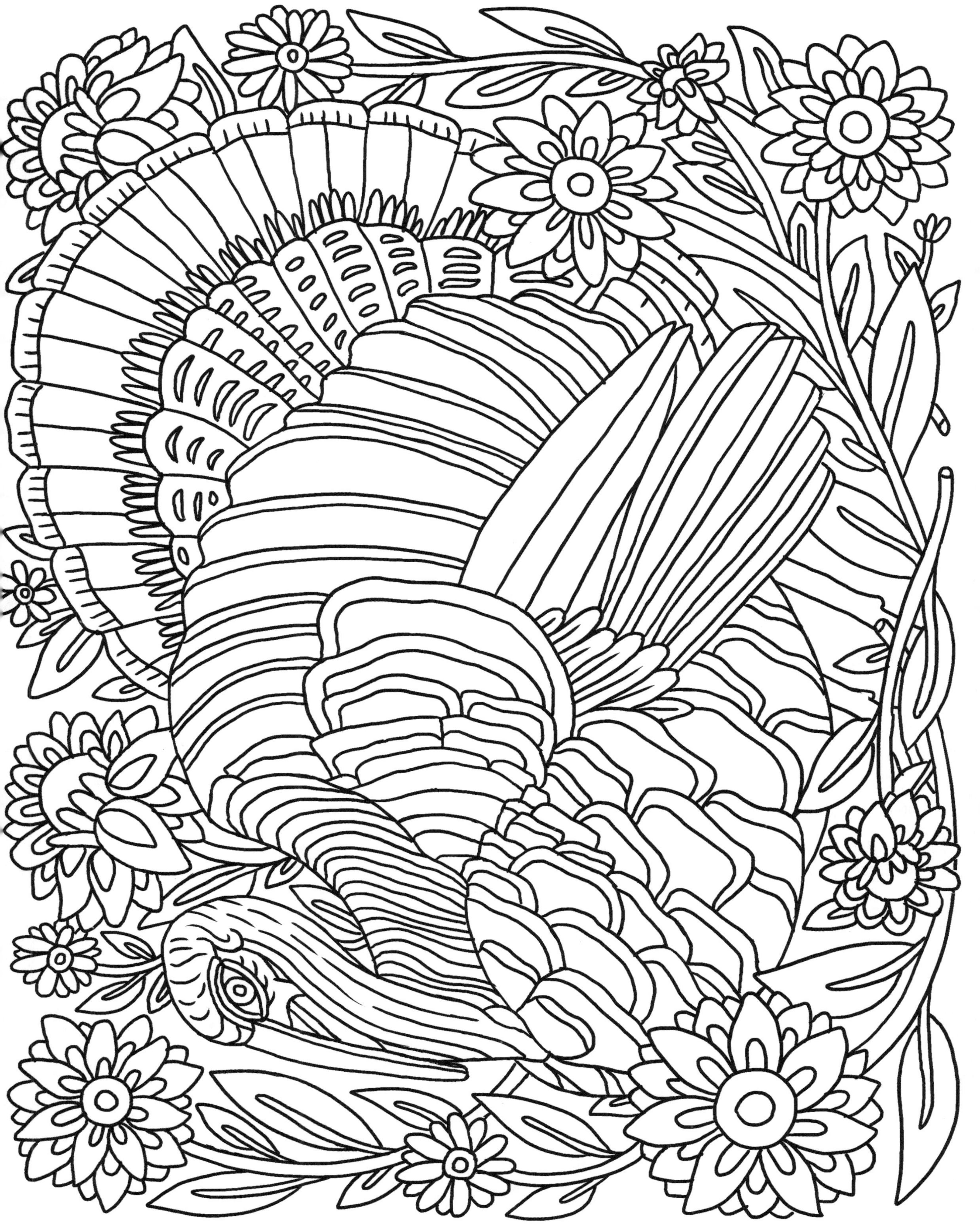

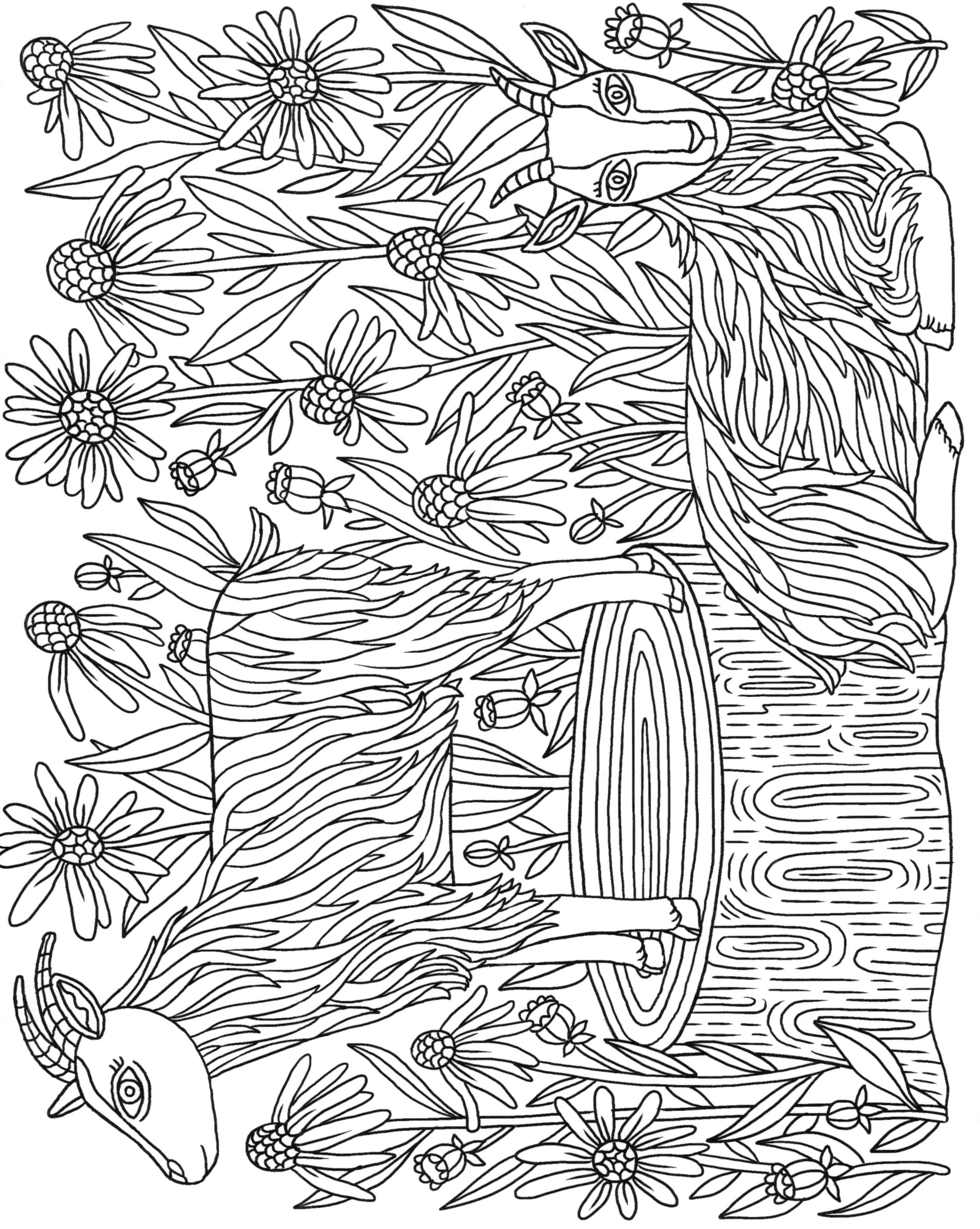

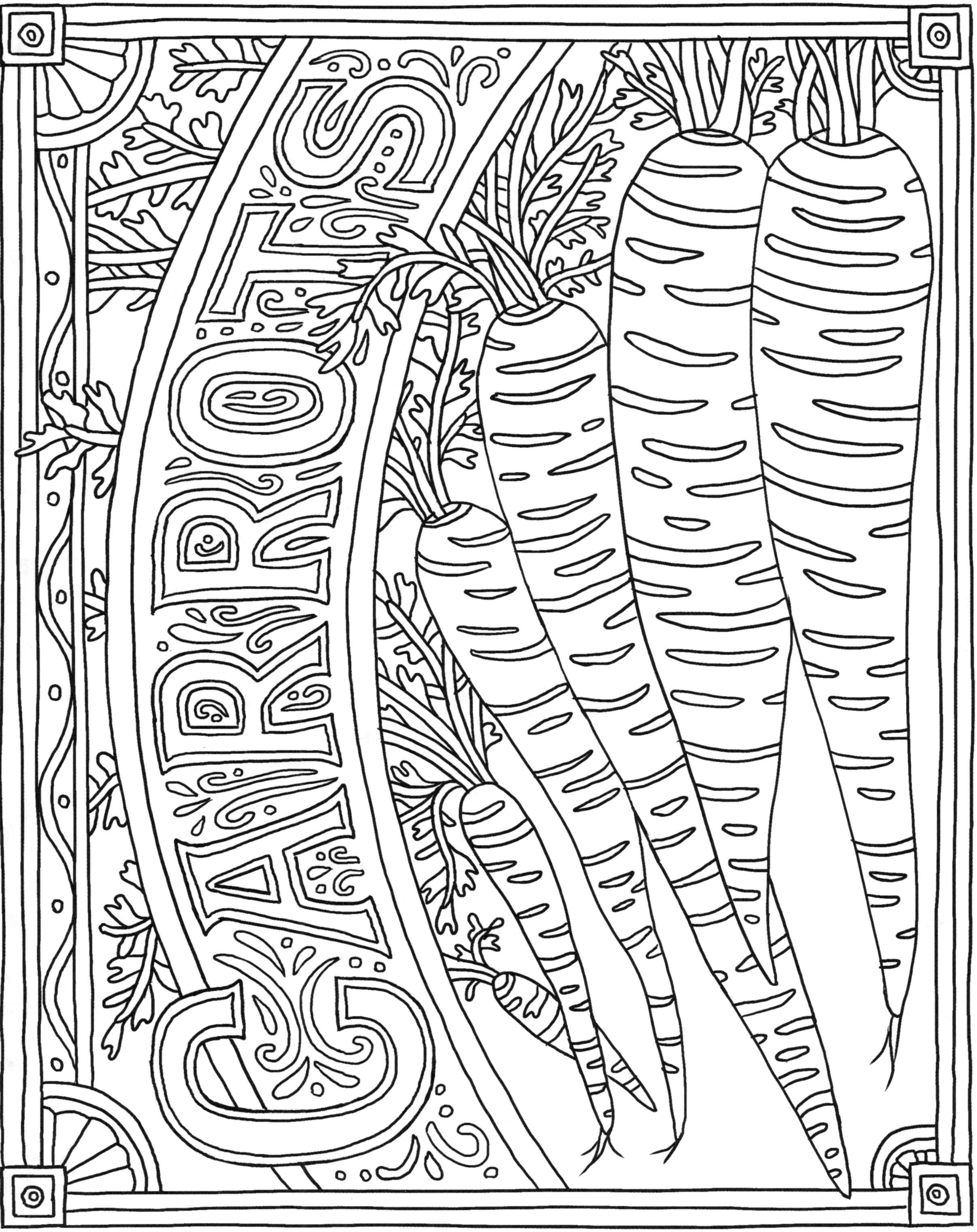
CARROTS

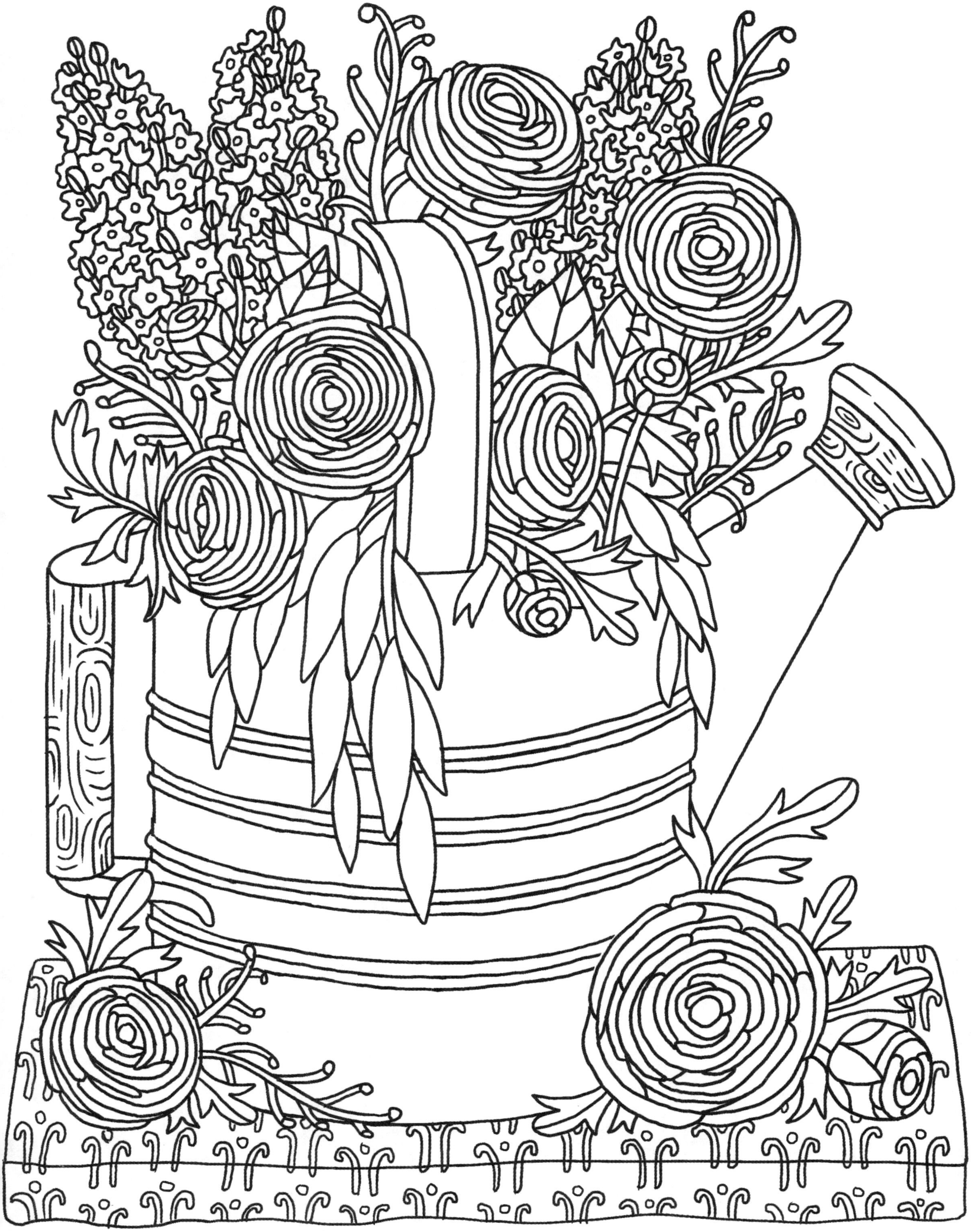

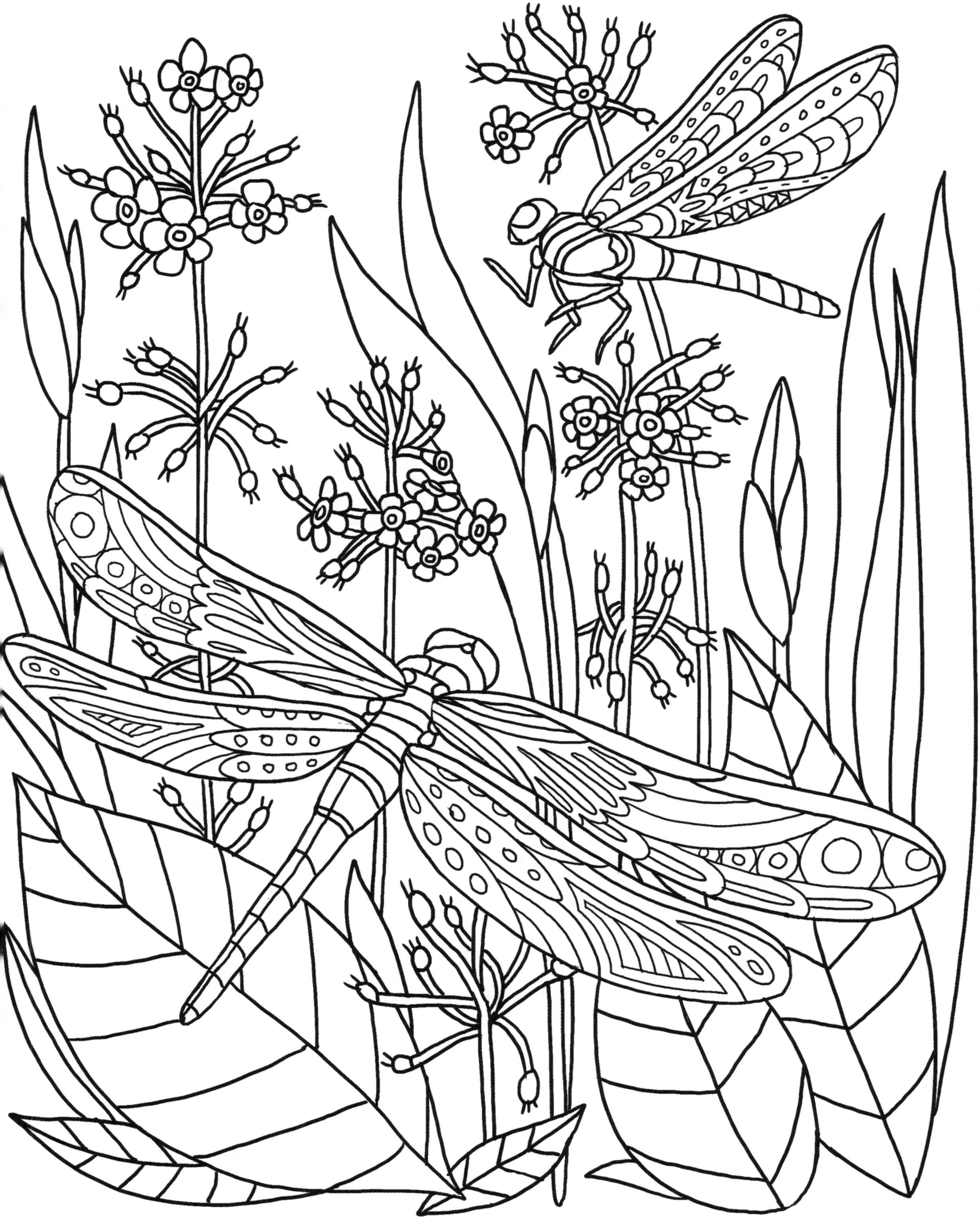

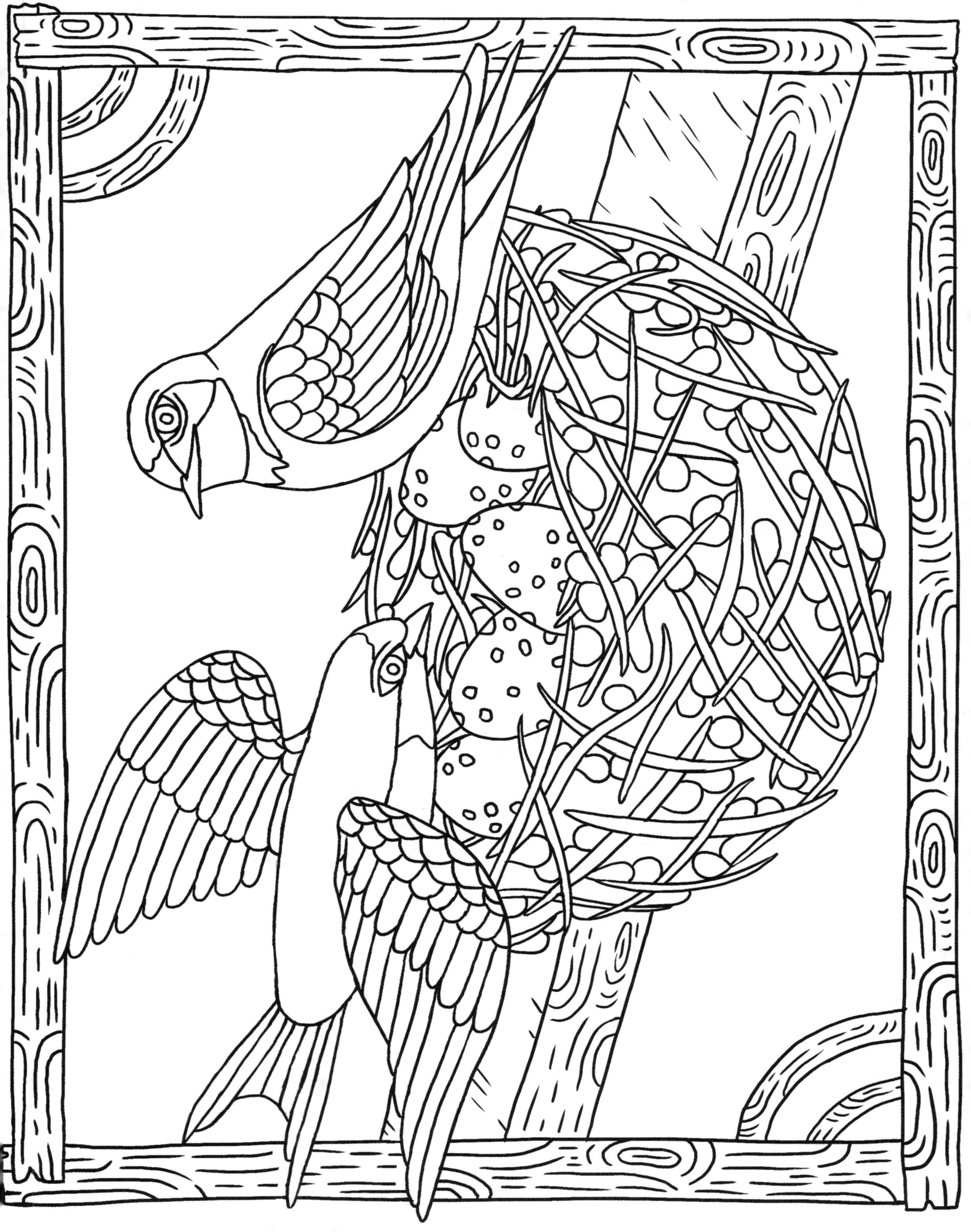

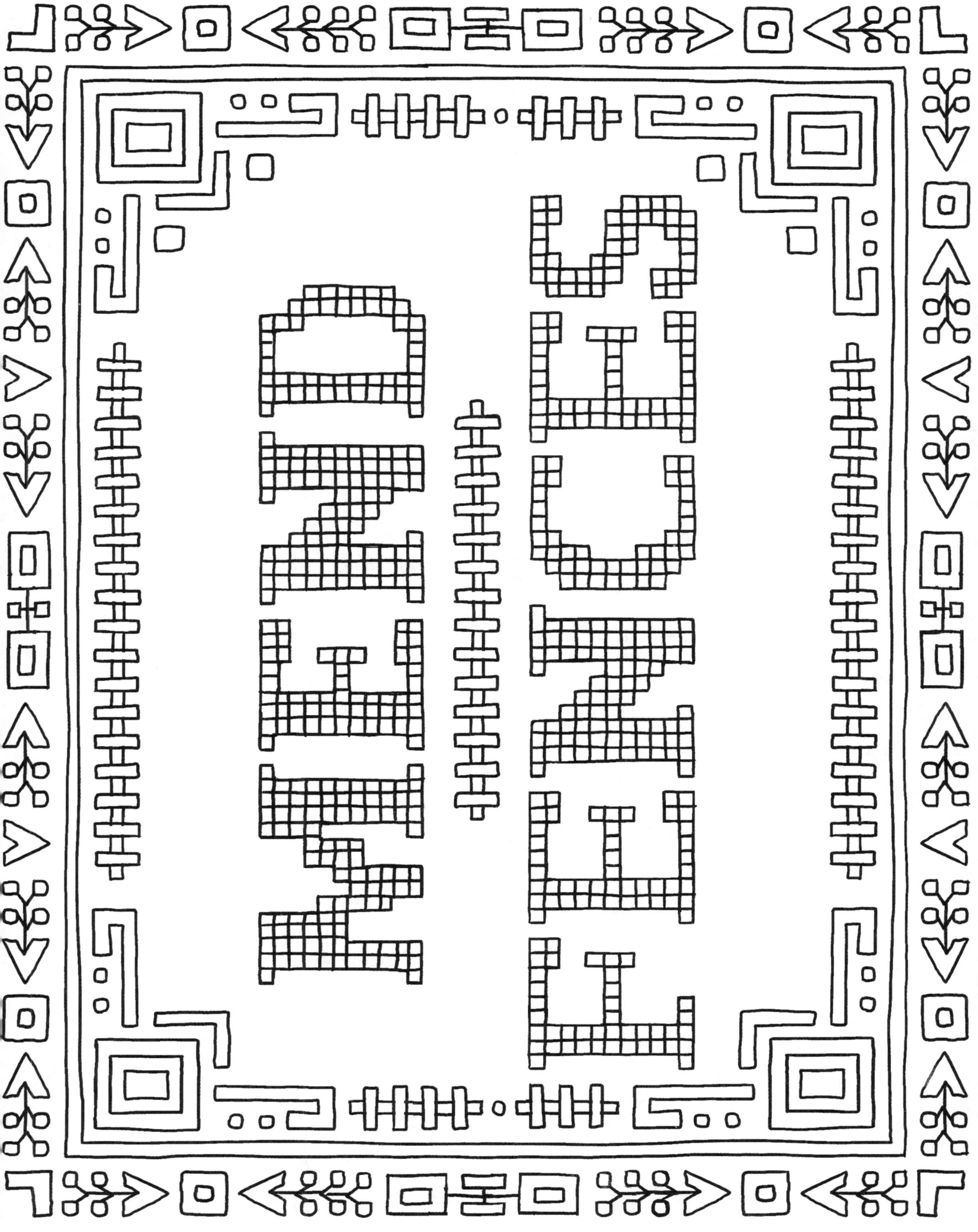
MEND
FENCES

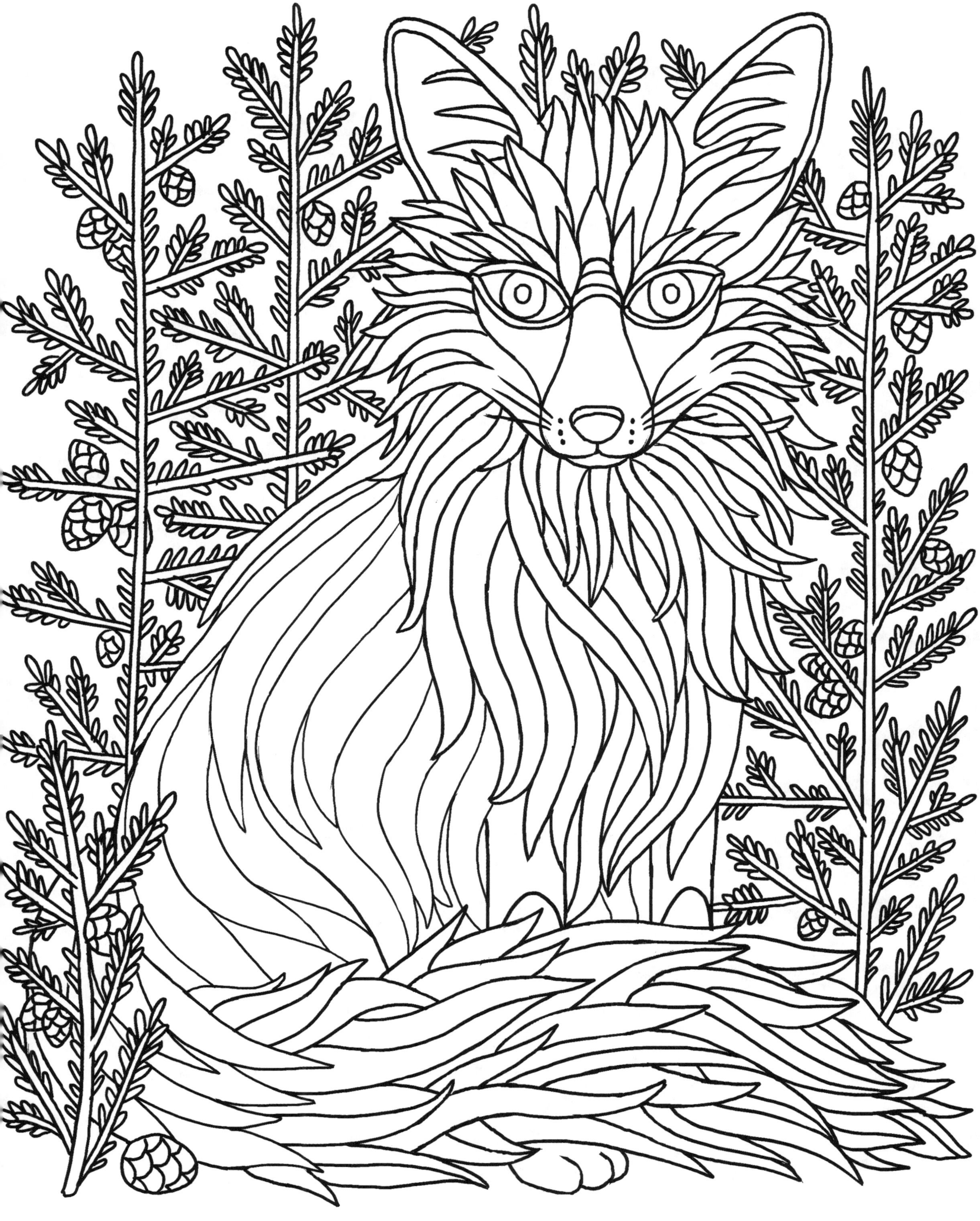

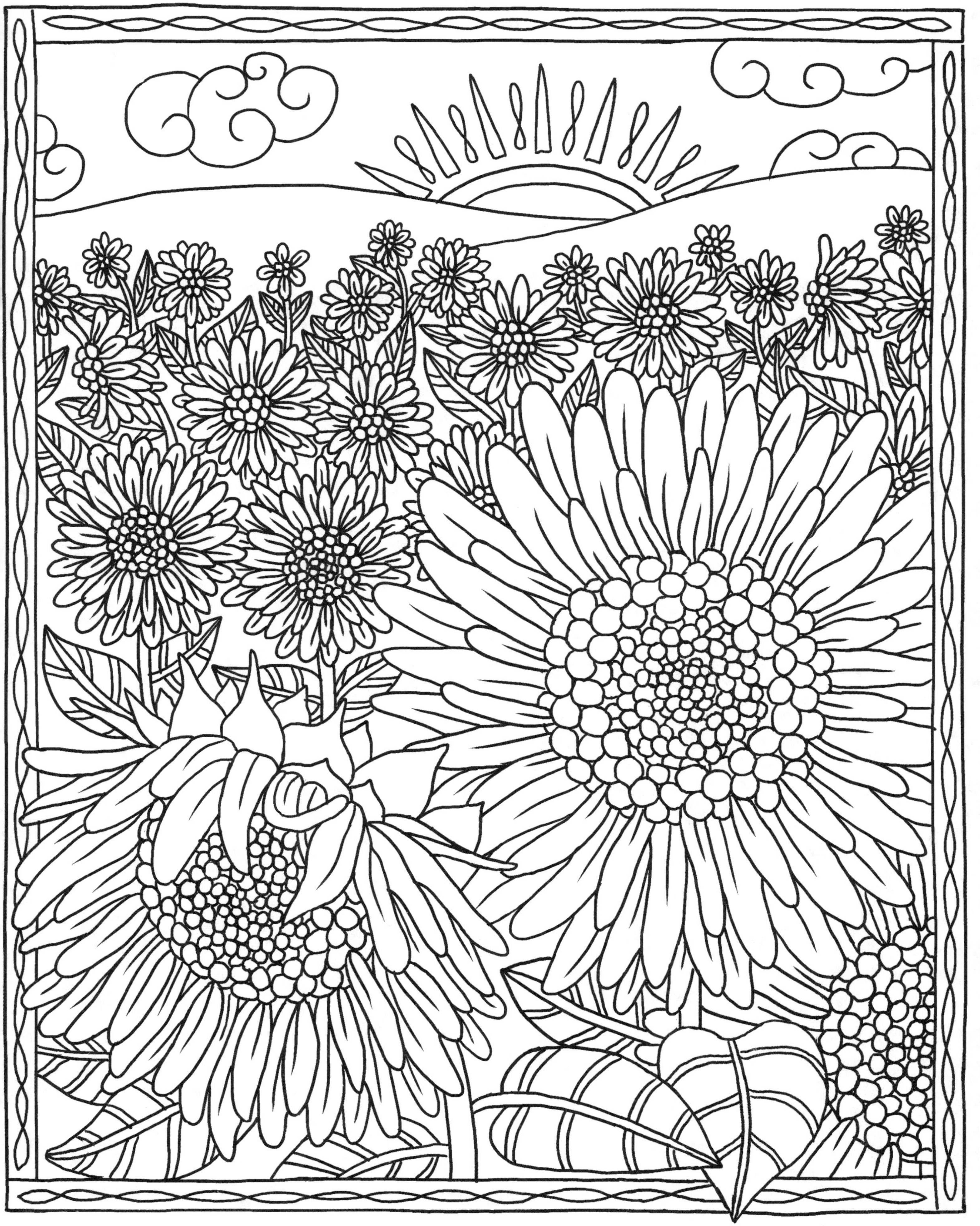

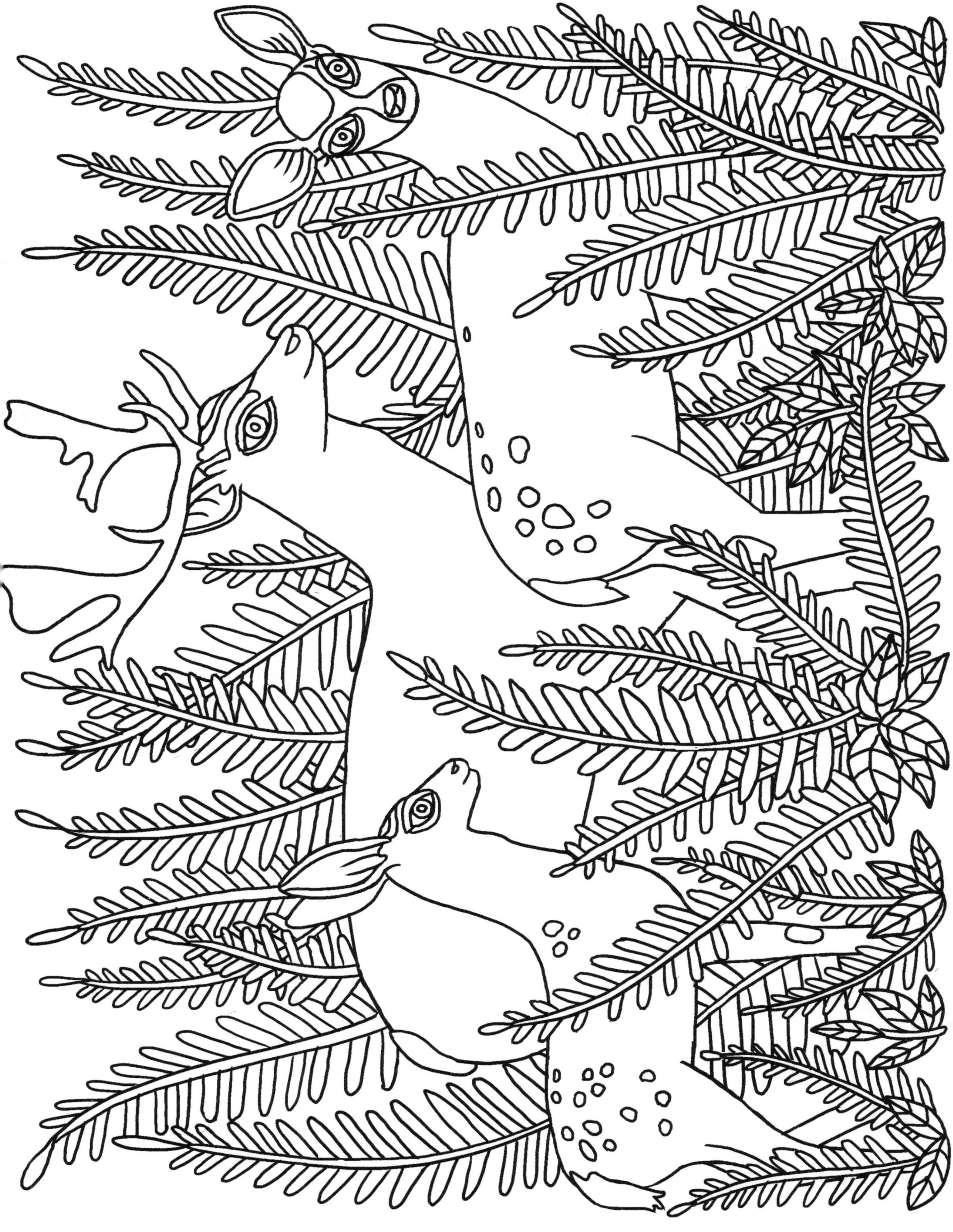

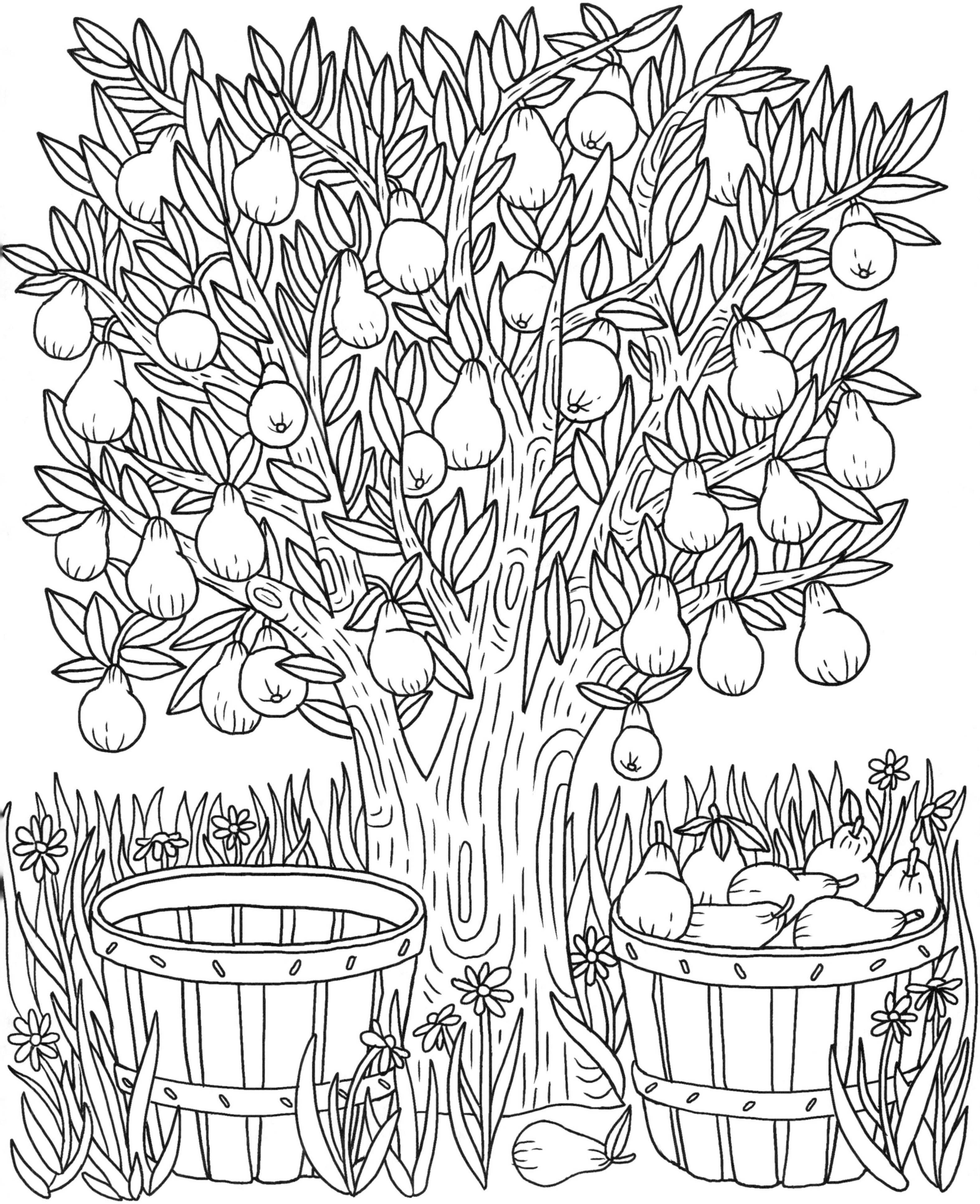

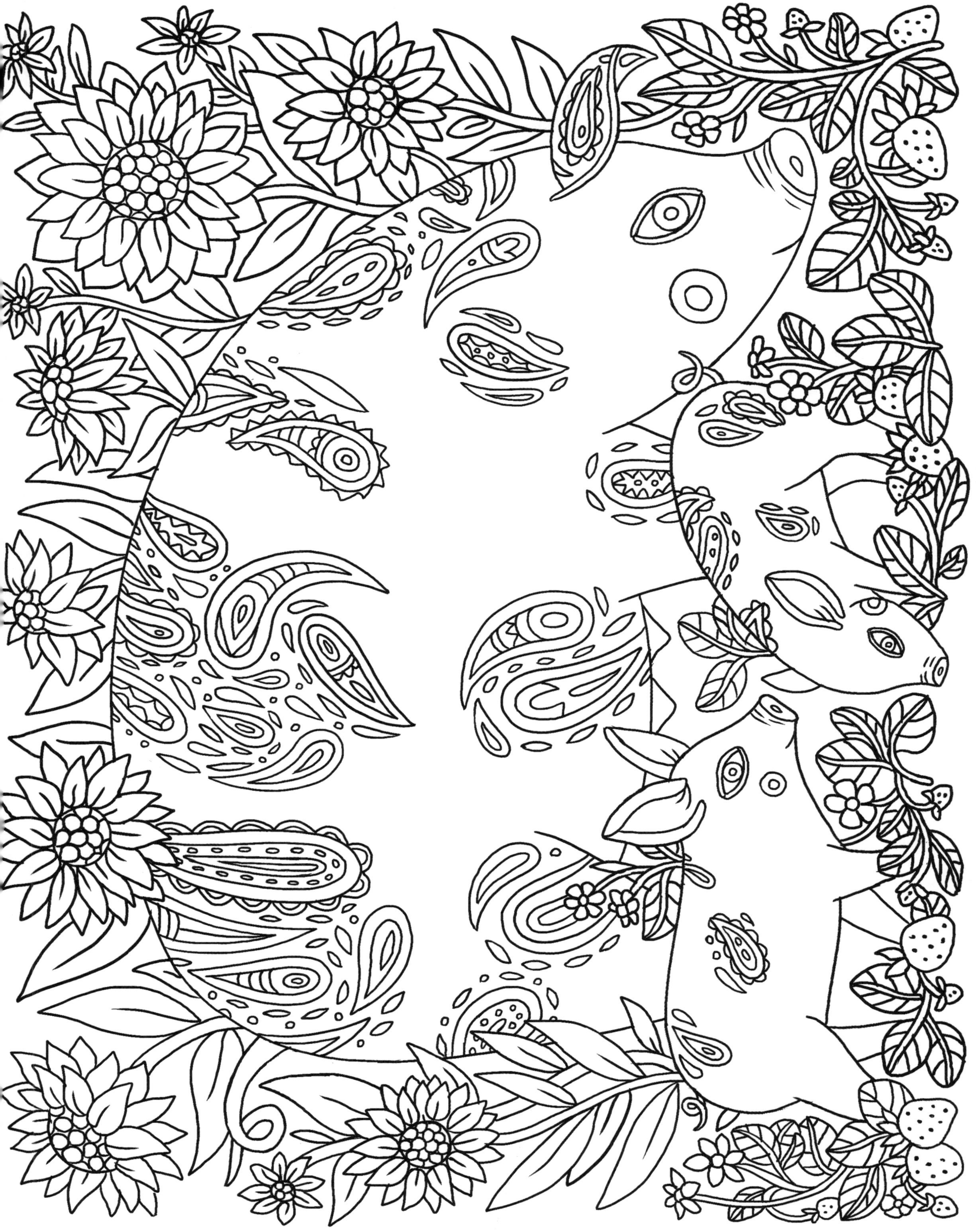

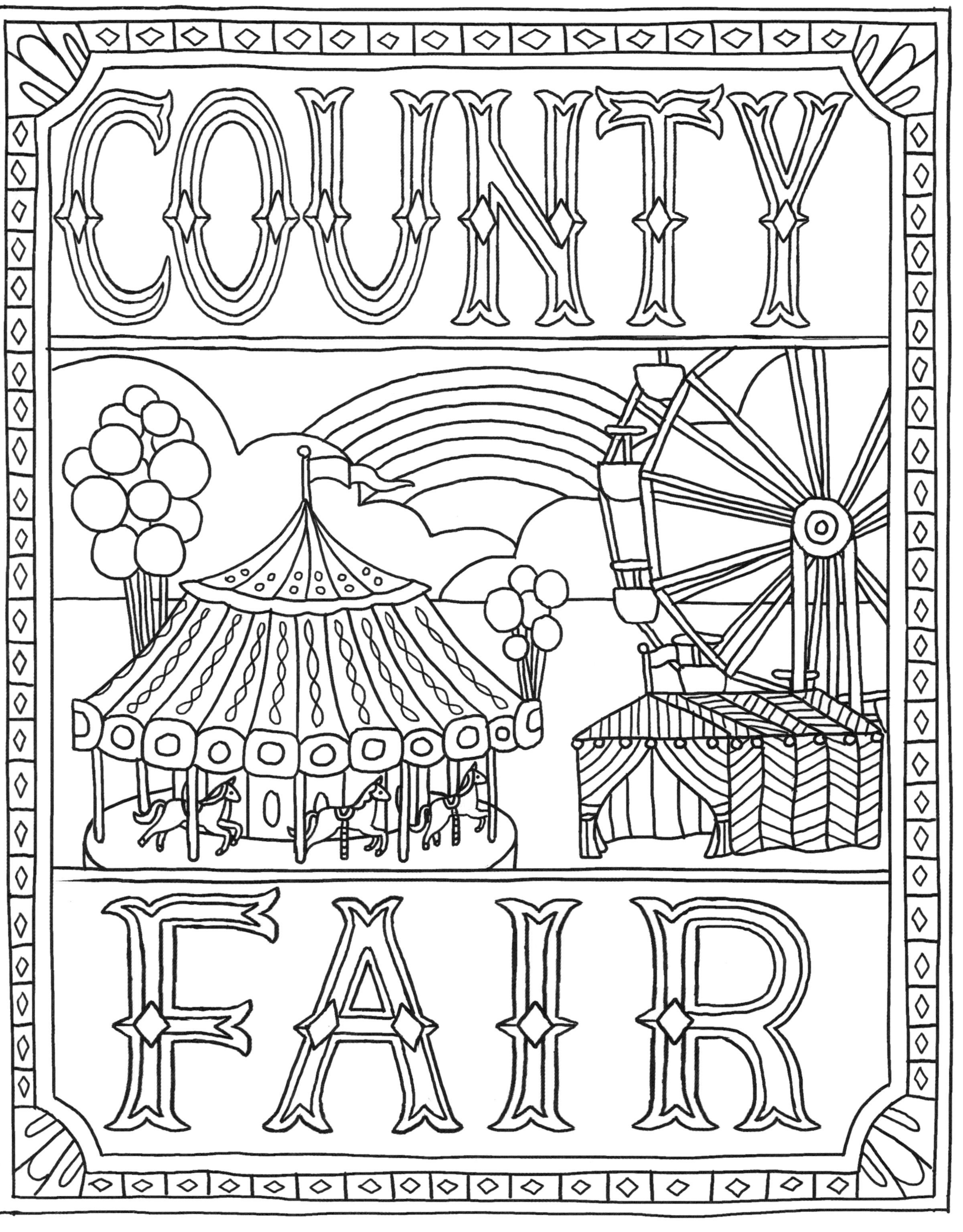
COUNTY
FAIR

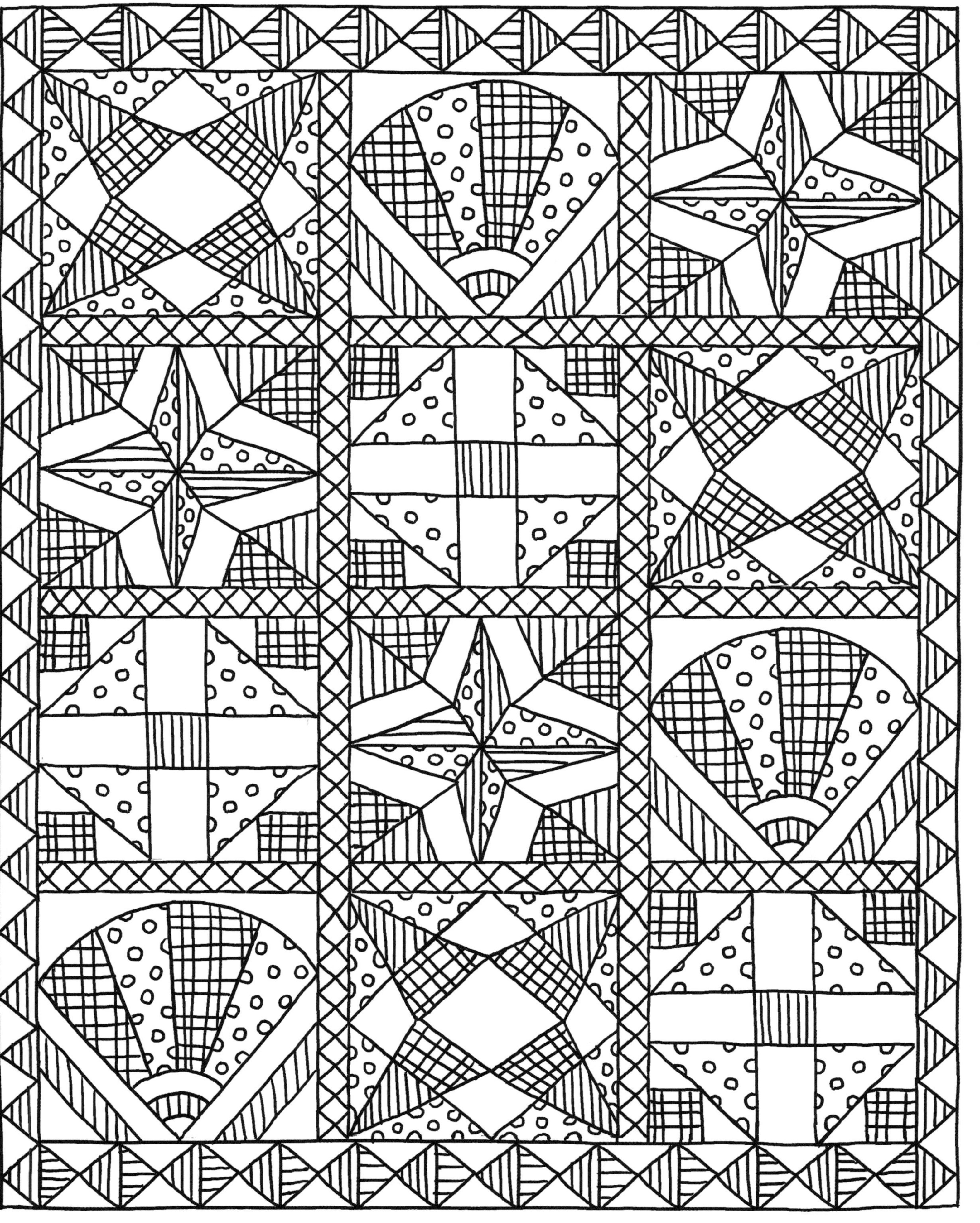

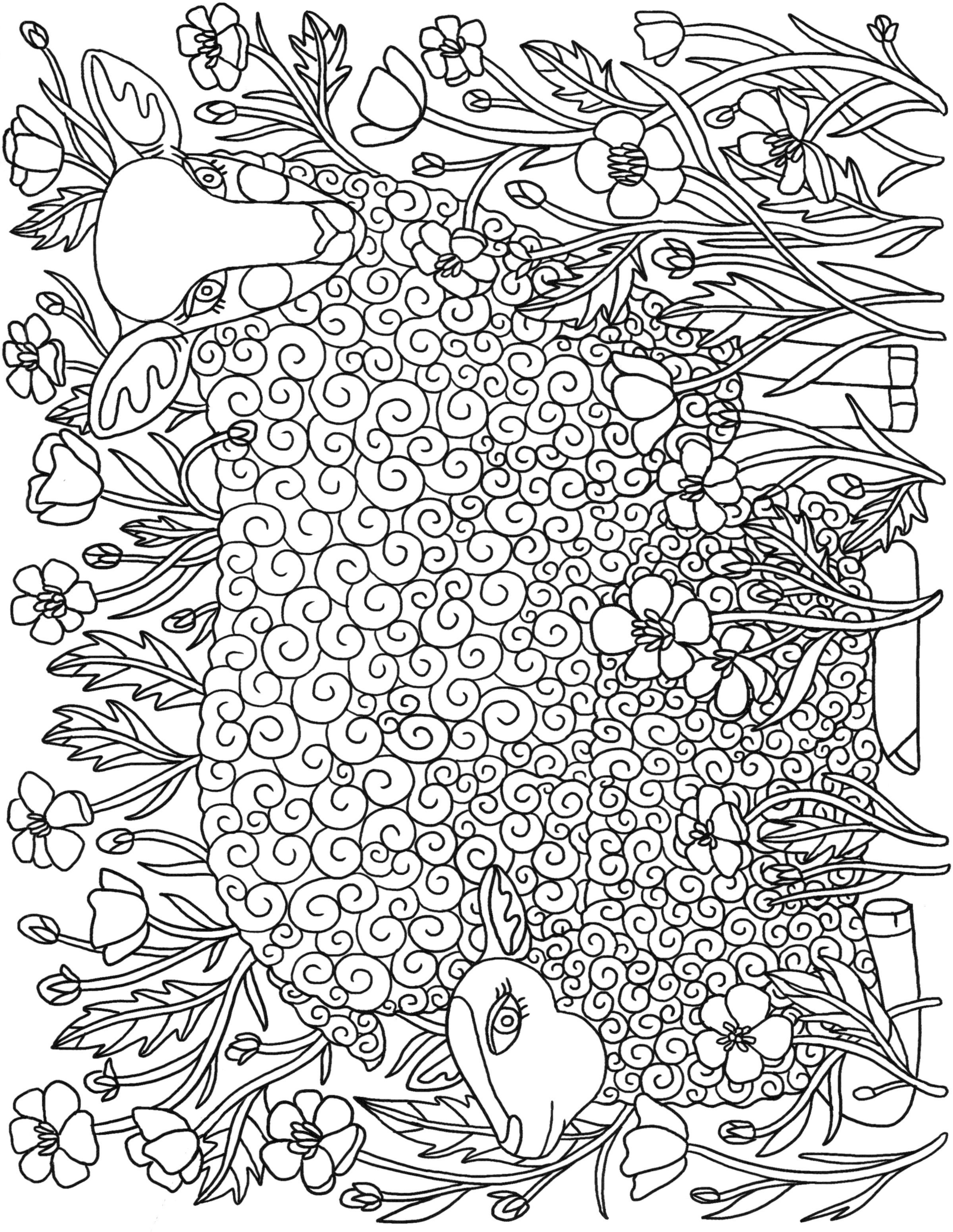

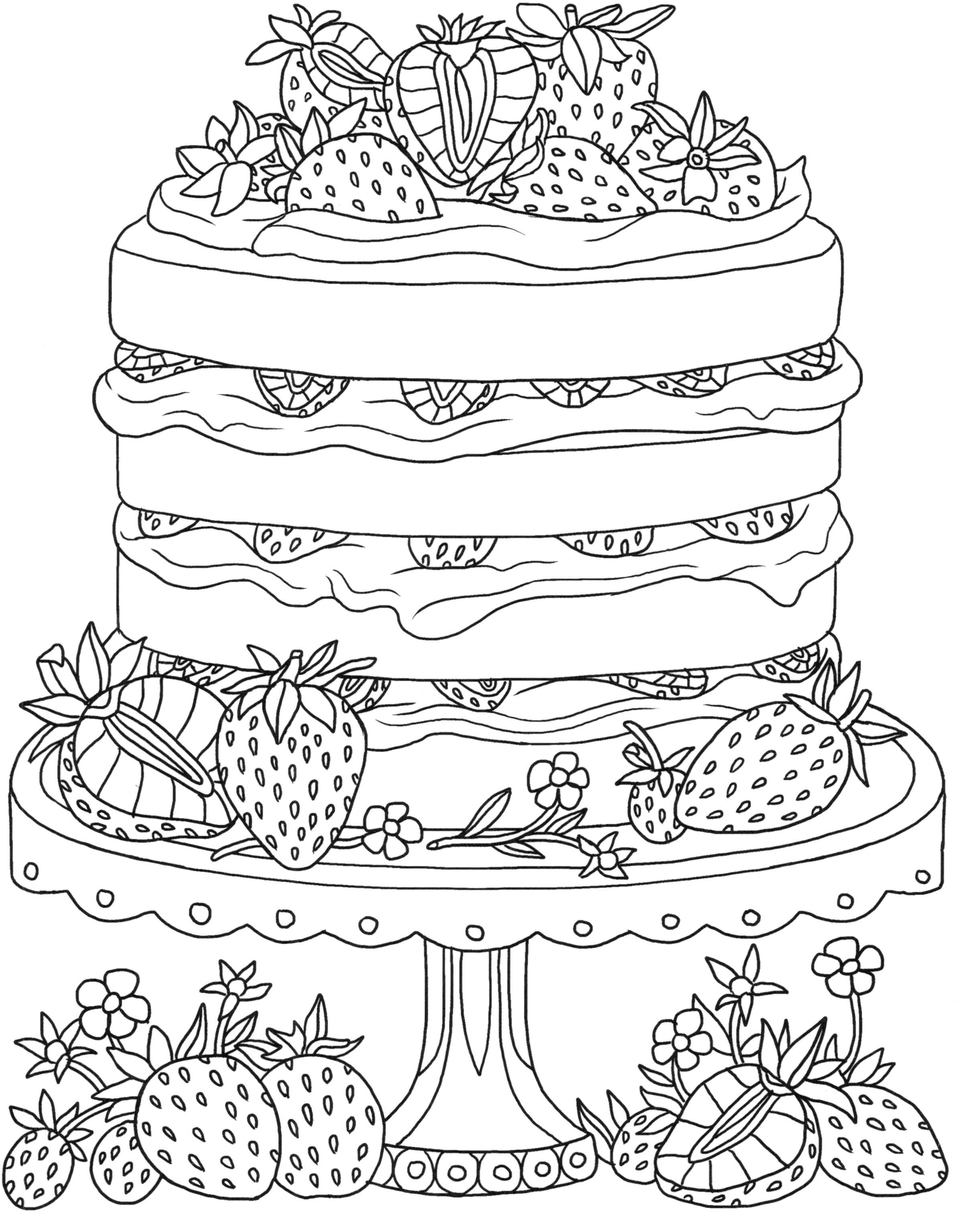

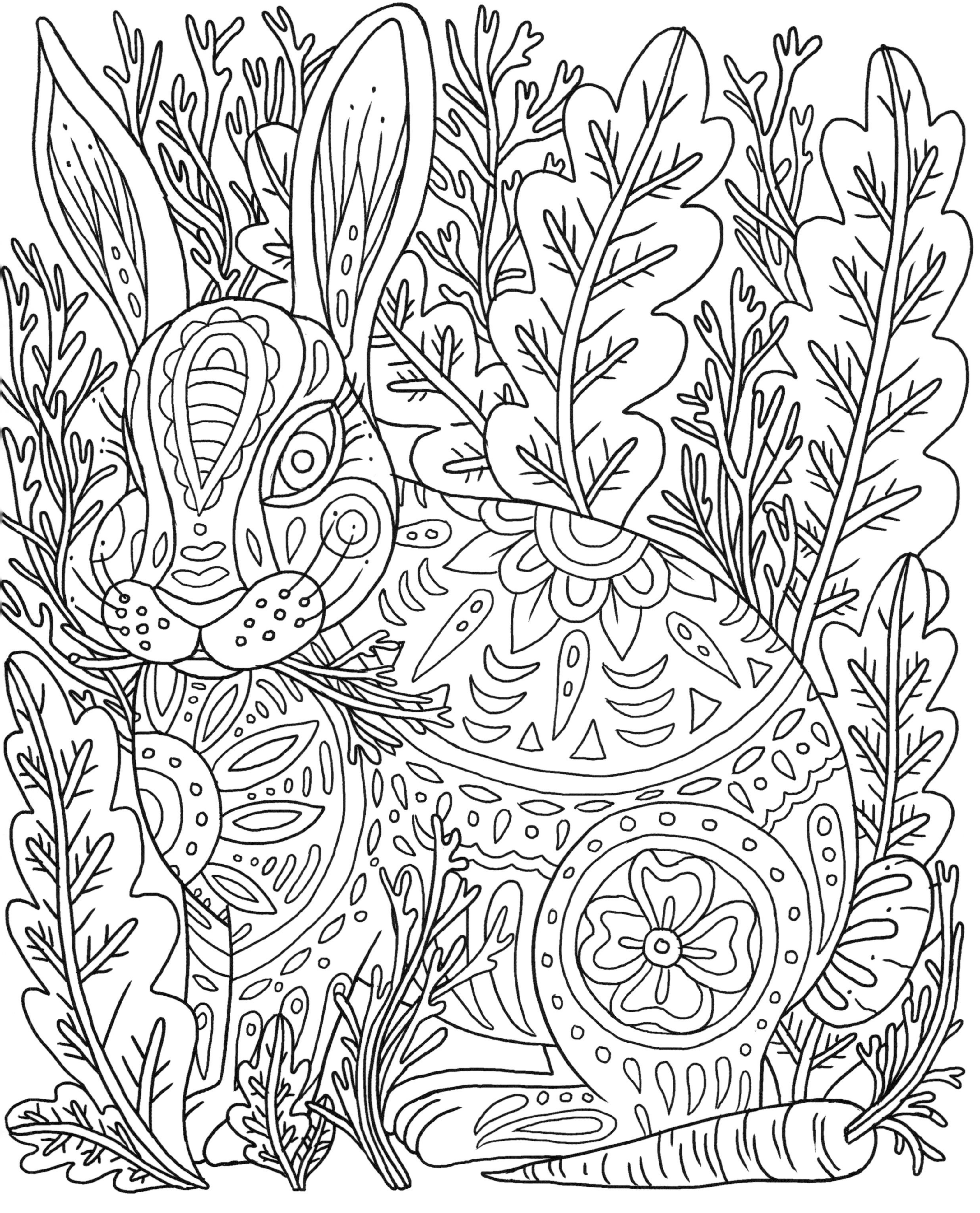

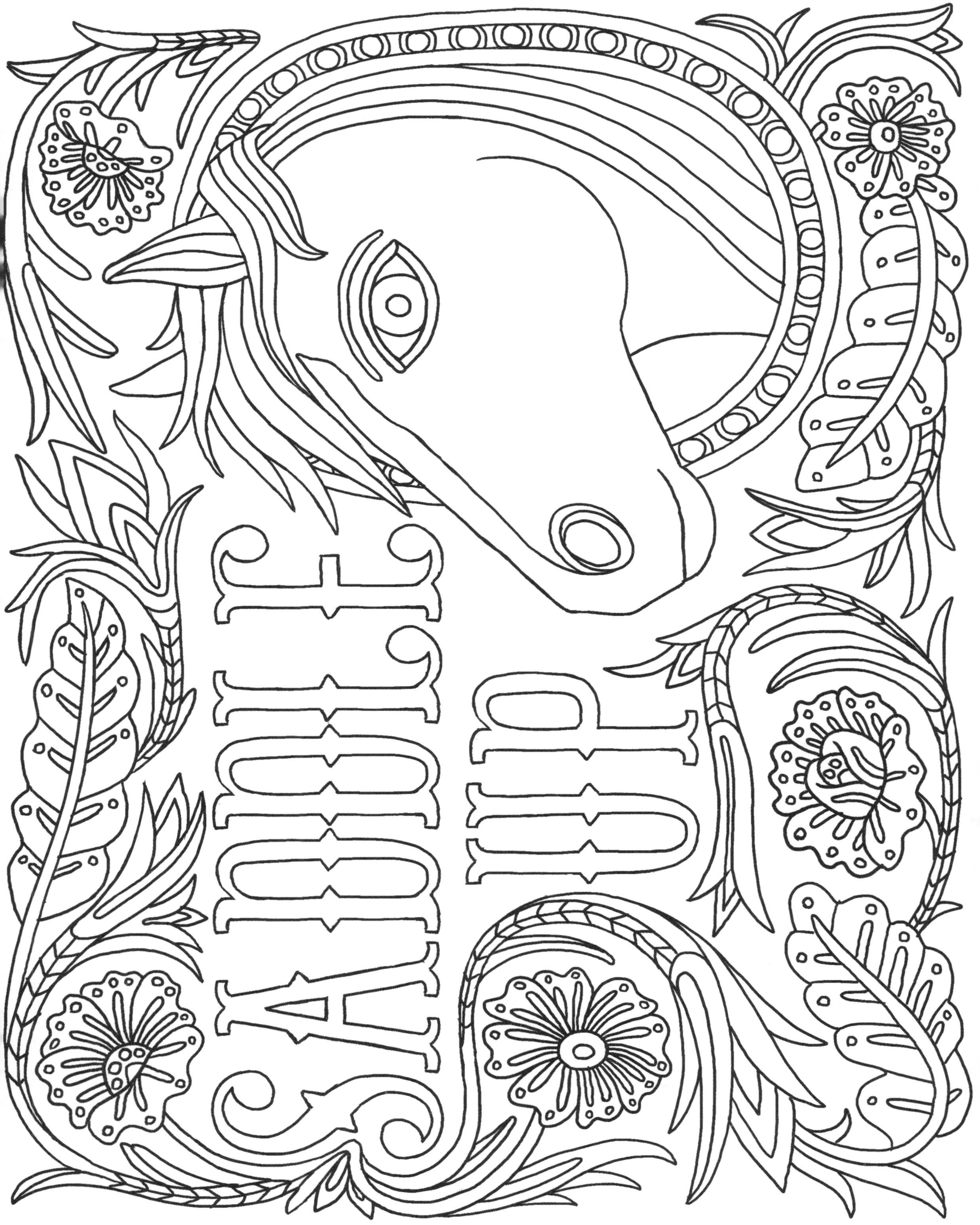
Saddle up

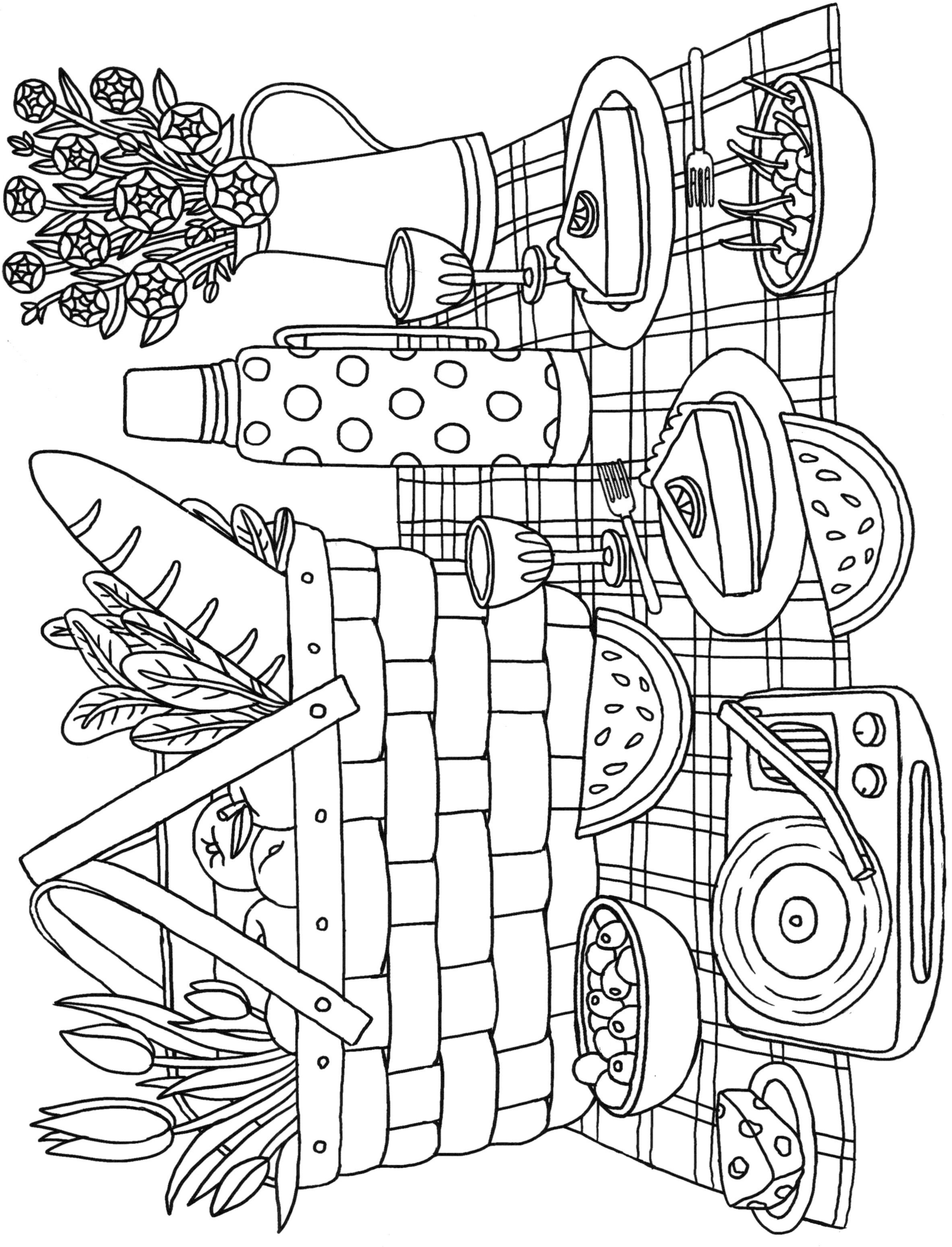

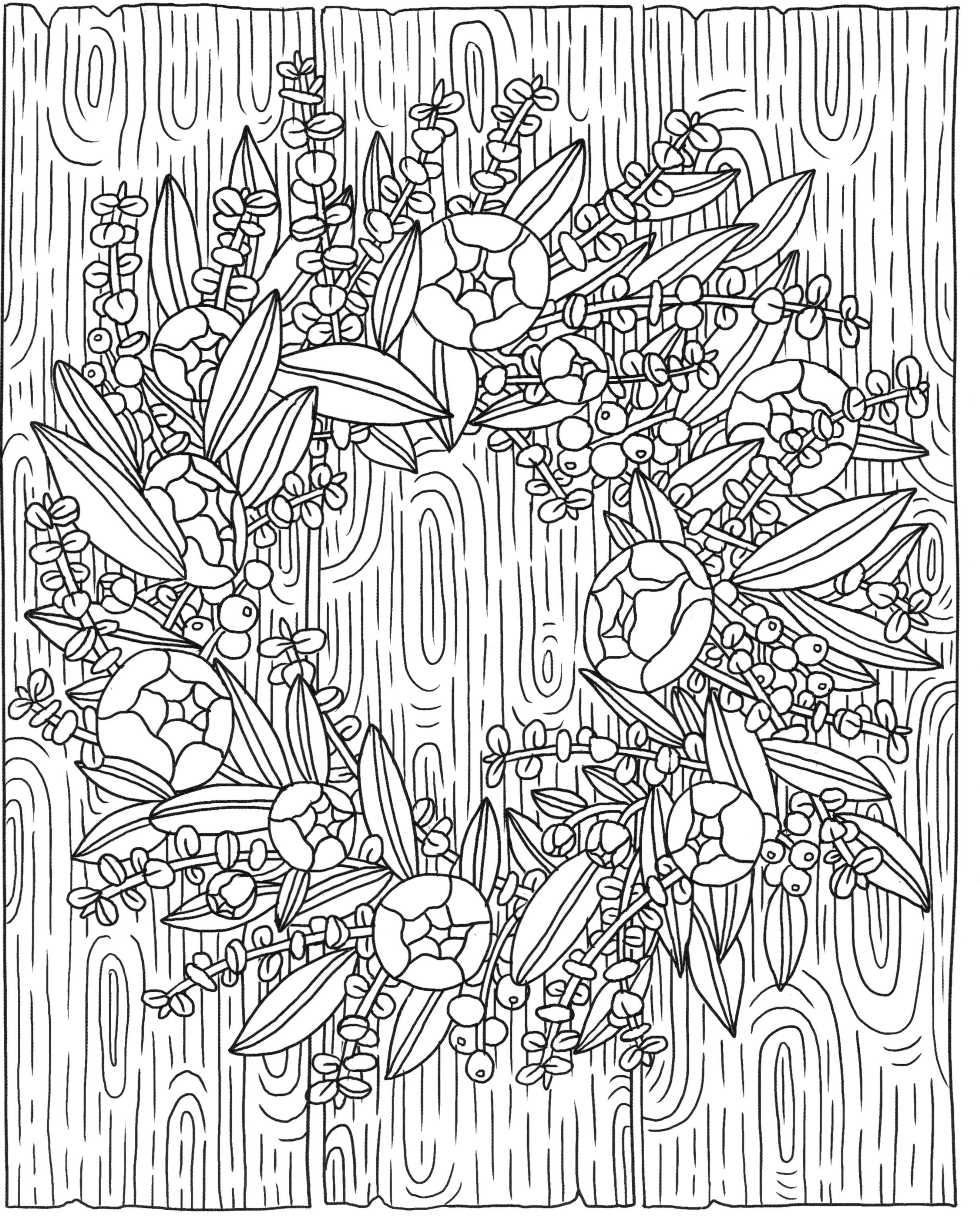